Raven

Ed Adams

a firstelement production

First published in Great Britain in 2020 by firstelement
Copyright © 2020 Ed Adams
Directed by thesixtwenty

10 9 8 7 6 5 4 3 2
All rights reserved.

No part of this publication may be reproduced, stored in a retrieval system, or transmitted, in any form or by any means, without the prior permission in writing of the publisher, nor be otherwise circulated in any form or binding or cover other than that in which it is published and without a similar condition including this condition being imposed on the subsequent purchaser.

Every effort has been made to acknowledge the appropriate copyright holders. The publisher regrets any oversight and will be pleased to rectify any omission in future editions.

Similarities with real people or events is unintended and coincidental.

The Owens Edition

A CIP catalogue record for this book is available from the British Library.

ISBN 13 : 978-1-8380146-7-4

eBook ISBN : 978-1-8380146-8-1

Printed and bound in Great Britain by Ingram Spark

rashbre
an imprint of firstelement.co.uk
rashbre@mac.com

Mailing list: https://mailchi.mp/9f0b30712620/ed_adams

To Terry and Marilyn

THANKS

A big thank you for the tolerance and bemused support from all of those around me. To those who know when it is time to say, " step away from the keyboard!" and to those who don't.

To thesixtwenty.co.uk for direction.

To the NaNoWriMo gang for the continued inspiration and encouragement.

To John, for many hours of intense scrutiny, whilst I was delicately scoffing asparagus.

To the symbol seers and adepts everywhere.

To my compadres across the years, in Austin, Texas

And, of course, thanks to the extensive support via the random scribbles of rashbre via http://rashbre2.blogspot.com and its cast of amazing and varied readers whether human, twittery, smoky, cool kats, photographic, dramatic, musical, anagrammed, globalized or simply maxed-out.

Not forgetting the cast of characters involved in producing this; they all have virtual lives of their own.

And of course, to you, dear reader, for at least 'giving it a go'.

Books by Ed Adams include:

- **The Triangle:** Dirty money? Here's how to clean it

- **The Square:** Weapons of Mass Destruction – don't let them get on your nerves

- **The Circle:** The desert is no place to get lost

- **The Ox Stunner:** *The Triangle Trilogy* – thick enough to stun an ox

- **Coin:** Get rich quick with Cybercash – just don't tell GCHQ

- **Pulse:** Want more? Just stay away from the edge

- **Edge:** Power can't be left to trust

- **Archangel :** Sometimes I am necessary

- **Raven:** An eye that sees all between darkness and light

SOMETHING ABOUT THE OTHER NOVELS

Summary of storylines:

Triangle trilogy
Triangle - About money laundering within an international setting.
Square - About a viral nerve agent being shipped by terrorists and WMDs
Circle - In the Arizona deserts, with the Navajo; about missiles stolen from storage.
The Ox Stunner - the above three in one heavy book.

- all feature Jake, Bigsy, Clare, Chuck Manners.

Linked with the Triangle:

Archangel - a biographical account of Russian trained Archangel, who, as Christina Nott, threads her way through other Triangle novels.

Raven: Big business gone bad and being a freemason won't absolve you

Stand-alone novels:

Coin - About cyber cash manipulation by the Russian state.
Pulse - Sci-Fi dystopian blood management with nano-bots
Edge - World end climate collapse and sham is discovered during magnetite mining from a Jupiter's moon Ganymede

Raven

TABLE OF CONTENTS

PART ONE   1

The setup   2
  Providence at a top table in London   3
  Rammed   4
  Carlton   7

London   12
  Boxpark   13
  Fortunes   15
  Put us in the corner 'cause we're into ideas   24
  Getting a grip   27
  Raven   29
  Philomena's   35
  Sfogliatelle   38

The Triangle   49
  Christina Hyde   50
  Clone a phone   55
  Burner   59

Freemasons   62
  Meet the Freemasons   63
  Handler   65
  Connections   68
  Eight Mechanisms   72

Box of Daylight   80
  Look around Raven   81
  Politics in big fat cars   85
  Amanda Miller   89
  J Sheekey   91
  Mondrian   94

Stuttgart — 96
- Triangle Works — 97
- Böblingen — 101
- Café Frech — 104
- Oskar's tale. — 108
- Poor Nelson — 112

Ask the Russians — 114
- A place by the lake — 115
- Echterdingen — 122
- London, the Triangle offices. — 124

Ladies' Night — 128
- Infiltrate — 129
- Handshakes — 132
- The Corruption of Bernard Driscoll — 143
- Masonic friends — 146
- Mystery address at the dome — 151

Chuck — 159
- 'Bin a long time — 160
- Fake News — 165
- Excuse — 170
- Amanda calls Chuck — 175
- Acacia — 177

PART TWO — 179

When we all fall asleep, where do we go? — 180
- Iraq news report — 181
- Burghers — 184
- Time for Stetsons? — 188

Texas — 193
- I'll need to get a bigger camera — 194

Frozen Margaritas machine	196
Austin, Texas	202
Raven Headquarters	204
Compound	213
What did we learn?	215
Touchdown	218

Primal Barrier — 221
- Antanov Analysis — 222
- Warp-speed farewell — 224
- Accessories — 226
- Cohiba — 232
- The American Station — 241
- Tap on the window — 244

PART THREE — 248

Secret Agent — 249
- Diversion — 250
- The clean-up — 258
- Anne-Maria Bristow — 261
- Snake-look leather belt — 265

Listening Station — 268
- Magpie — 269
- Young — 278
- Blackbird calling — 281
- Vauxhall Cross — 283

Chairman of the Board — 286
- Raven Board Meeting — 287
- Grace Cathedral Hill — 298
- Fake 'n ham — 302
- Berry — 306
- Occupational hazards — 310

Chuck gets out of Dodge	314

Driscoll Shining — **317**
Soft power	318
The Offer	324
Parliamentary Debate	327
The Launch	334
Financial Times	337

Four Theories and a Funeral — **340**
The Riverside	341
Popups	346
Vzyatochnichestvo	349
Gavvers	352
Wrap it up	363
Loud and clear	367

PART ONE

The Eye of Providence is a symbol,
having its origin in Christian iconography,
showing an eye often surrounded by
rays of light or a glory
and usually
enclosed
by

a
triangle.

It represents
the concept of
divine providence.

The setup

Among all you angels is a champion angel
Among all you devils there's a free soul
Up from the disenfranchised the engine cries
Up from the circle there's a hole

Benjamin Knox Miller / Jeffrey Carl Prystowsky /
Jocelyn Jager Adams

Providence at a top table in London

It was a busy reception. Drinks, canapés, a few celebrities, including some A-listers. Piano and guitar songs from a well-known pop-idol. An inspirational speech from a member of the Chiefs rugby team.

Off to the side was a compact room. In different times they would have filled it with cigar smoke. Nowadays just the dark-suited men.

"We're going to need Brant, " said one.

The others nodded.

"Make it look like a ship of fools, " said a second voice.

"Yes, it is my little indulgence, " said the first voice, " We can rotate the staffing after we have positioned the deals."

"Who can we use to position it?" asked the second voice.

"Someone who hasn't sipped at Mimir's Well. Someone we can control. A puppet."

"I have the very person, a clean skin, " said a third voice.

"Well, let's invite him into the club." Said the first voice, as if concluding the discussion.

Rammed

The small bar was crowded, yet they'd found a table.

Corporate away day and everyone had come to the same place, some spilling onto the Croisette.

"We'll be moving on?" asked Rizzo.

Lieke nodded, " Yes, this place is rammed with the sales boys, breathe in the testosterone."

There was a crash behind them as two suited men grappled with arm-wrestling, for some kind of bet. In another corner there was a loud quiz betting machine with around a dozen people crowded around it.

A few loud shouts across the noise - orders for drinks. And two intense people in front of them talking about trading algorithms.

"Ladies, " said a voice, " May I join you?" A smiling suited repster was walking towards them.

"We were just leaving, " smiled Rizzo back. Rizzo - Elena

Ricci, was from the Milan office. This junket to the south of France was an eye-opener in more ways than one. It was supposed to be to entertain and educate clients, but by mid-evening had turned into a corporate drinking fest.

Lieke stood and put on her leather jacket. She nodded towards the door of the bar. Rizzo picked up her bag and joined Lieke. The charm of the suit in front of her hadn't worked, but she noticed he was also calling to a couple of his mates who were in the process of taking over the table they had vacated.

Lieke shuddered outside the bar. "We work for that organisation, yet the main sales force are like predatory animals, " she said.

Rizzo nodded agreement, " Yes, do you think we'll become like that if we stay with the company long enough?"

"I hope not, " answered Lieke, " It's a scary thought."

"Although they always say that without those people we'd not get paid because we'd have no clients, " answered Rizzo. She was looking along the road for a taxi and at just that moment one appeared.

"Shall we go back?" she asked Rizzo.

"Yes, " replied Rizzo, " It'll be quieter at the hotel."

They gave their instructions to the taxi driver. Lieke spoke French to the driver, although she wondered if his grasp of the language was less than hers.

The driver sat on a wooden massage seat cover and took the long way back to the hotel, along the Promenade missing the nearest turn-around and driving significantly further before changing direction.

'No cards', it said inside the taxi, 'Cash only'

They arrived back at the Carlton, a few minutes away.

"Quatorze euros, " said the taxi driver.

Lieke handed over a twenty euro note.

"No change, " said the driver, in English.

Rizzo was onto him. She called over the doorkeeper from the Carlton.

"He's got no change and wants to charge us an extra six, " she said in English.

The liveried doorman bent down towards the driver's window. The driver looked under the passenger seat and magically found his leather bag with loose change.

He counted out three two-euro coins.

Lieke took the money and climbed out.

"Godverdomme, " she said in her native Dutch, " wat een plek, geramde bars en overvallers. Klootzakken."

Rizzo didn't understand but laughed. "I agree, she said, " With all of that."

Carlton

"One more?" asked Rizzo.

"Yes, it's still early, " said Lieke.

The ambiance inside the Carlton was altogether different from the rammed bar they had left. They spied a table and sat down. Cool prestige emanated from the bar and its clientele.

"I can understand why Grace Kelly used to come here, " said Rizzo.

"Hi Lieke, " said a voice behind them. They turned to look.

Lieke immediately stood and smiled, " Hey Nelson, I didn't expect to see you here."

They kissed one another on the cheeks, in the Dutch way. He looked to Rizzo, " I don't think we've met?"

"Hi, " said Rizzo, " Elena Ricci, from the Milan office. I

think we've met by phone and email!"

"Hi Elena, it's great to put a face to a name! And thank you - from me personally - for those complicated predicaments you've saved me from in the past!"

"Do you mind if I join you? I've been deserted by the gang. They all wanted to go to some rowdy bar along the Croisette."

"Please do, it'll be good to hear what's happening in London. How's the old bosses Liz and Ron getting on?" asked Lieke.

"Uh, they're doing fine, since they moved on, they've just set up a new shell - The Summerhouse. I think they are filling it with artworks and some kind of trainer project, " answered Nelson.

"Trainer project?" asked Lieke.

"Training, yeah, you know the kind of thing. Expensive and many types, if I remember correctly, " replied Nelson, " I'd forgotten that you knew them."

The waiter appeared, " Gin and tonic, " said Lieke.

"G-Kelly, " asked Rizzo.

"You know what, " said Lieke, " Make that G&T a Bombay Ultimate."

"Er - I'll have a San Pellegrino, " said Nelson.

"Saving yourself?" asked Lieke.

"Kind of, " said Nelson, " I was with a client earlier and

we drank too many Manhattans. It's a real killer."

"That and the mad prices in here, no wonder it's quiet. I could fly to Monaco by helicopter for the price of a round of drinks, " said Rizzo.

"That's why I swapped from a G&T to a cocktail, " said Lieke, " Might as well get the money's worth!"

"Don't worry, we'll charge them to my room, " said Nelson, " Time to get something back."

He grimaced and then leaned forward, " You haven't heard then?"

"No, what's happened!"

"What will happen more like."

"There's a few planning sessions running here alongside the main event. It turns out that part of the company is to be hived off to another one."

"I'm in the piece that is moving."

"We are no longer Raven; we'll be Brant Holdings."

"Brant?" asked Lieke, " I've never heard of them?"

"Exactly, " said Nelson, " It's a file and forget manoeuvre."

"What? They are shifting people out of the way?" asked Rizzo, " That's surely not legal, workers' right and all that."

"No, they have brought in one of those specialist firms to hack through the structure."

The drinks arrived.

"Wow, these look good, " said Lieke, " Er even your big bottle of San Pellegrino looks good with that glass, " she nodded towards a glass chilled with ice. See, they have given you two glasses, so that one can be chilled and then you can tip the ice into the other one!"

They chinked glasses and said, " Cheers!"

"Which piece is going then?" asked Lieke, " Not the whole London operation, surely?"

"No, they are being very selective. I think they are keeping the corporate trading division but losing the retail arm. It's supposed to be to do with profitability."

"We haven't heard about this in Amsterdam, " said Lieke.

"Nor us in Milan, " said Rizzo.

"To be honest, I smell a rat in all of this, " said Nelson, " There's something about this that doesn't add up. The money men have been crawling all over the situation, I think they are up to something bigger."

"So, what will you do?" asked Lieke.

"I've little choice but to move. I might just rack up some expenses here first though, " Nelson chuckled, " But seriously, I think there is something dodgy about what they are doing. Meetings on golf courses in Ireland, that type of thing."

"So, you think the company is up to no good? More than usual?" asked Lieke.

"Yes, but I don't know where to find out what's been happening."

They sipped their drinks.

"I know someone, " said Lieke, " She is living in Amsterdam, but I think she's originally from somewhere else. She seems to have a bit of a reputation as a corporate problem solver. And I think she knows people in London too. I think this is right up her street."

"Hold on though, won't she want to get paid for delving into a company?"

"Not necessarily, " said Lieke, " I think she finds prizes inside the companies. More a kind of Risk and Reward deal. I'm a good friend of hers, shall I ask her about it?"

"Well, it's all supposed to be a company secret at the moment, " said Nelson., " And I don't want to jeopardise my transfer fee."

"Christina can be very discreet, " said Lieke, " Let me talk to her about it in the vaguest of terms."

London

My mother was a Chinese trapeze artist
In pre-war Paris
Smuggling bombs for the underground.
And she met my father
At a fete in Aix-en-Provence.
He was disguised as a Russian cadet
in the employ of the Axis.

And there in the half-light
Of the provincial midnight
To a lone concertina
They drank in cantinas
And toasted to Edith Piaf
And the fall of the Reich.

Colin Meloy

Boxpark

Christina was in London when Elena called from Cannes.

"Hi, I was just on my way to the Spitalfields Boxpark, " she said, " Time for some renewal."

Elena smiled, " I didn't even know you were in London, "

"And I didn't know you were in Cannes. What are you doing there? A boy? Vacation? Or is it work?"

"Yes, it's work, loud and shouty, " answered Elena, " Het is zo verdomd saai - het zijn allemaal cretins."

"I always thought that about your co-workers, at least the ones that I got to meet, " answered Christina, switching back to English.

"Well, it looks as if there's something else happening to the company now, some kind of weird deal. Raven is going to sell off part of itself to another organisation called Brant Holdings.

"Some of my friends are being transferred away. It's

being planned from London as far as I can tell. I was wondering if you'd take a little look. My friend Nelson thinks there is more to it than meets the eye."

"Interesting., " said Christina, " Why would he say that?"

"Put it this way, " Raven always has a reputation for sailing close to the wind, we reckon it might be trying to cover something up this time."

"Let me think about it, " said Christina, " If I say yes, do you want me to work alone, or can I bring in some friends?"

"I was hoping you'd ask that, " said Elena.

Fortunes

The Boxpark was bustling when Christina arrived. She knew her way around at what was considered to be the world's first pop-up shopping mall, built on containers stacked on top of one another.

She had arranged to meet some people at one of the bars, but before this was wondering about whether to browse a few of the small shops.

Then, she saw something that caught her eye. A fortune teller. She didn't believe in any of it but thought it would be good to try someone for ideas about what she'd just heard from Elena.

The inside of the container was a small room, heavily decorated with soft furnishings and a few pieces of ju-ju art. Across the way sat the fortune teller. She looked up as Christina approached. Christina realised that the teller was a man in drag.

"Hi, " she said, " I'm interested in a reading, " she smiled across at the teller, who she could see was slightly confused by her sleek appearance.

"Hello, " said the teller, affecting a mysterious Madame's voice.

"Look, " said Christina, " We can be friends if you like. Please drop the tourist act though."

"Okay, he said, " Can I dispense with the crystal ball too, I can see you don't need one?"

"No ball-shit here, please, " said Christina.

"You're the real deal, you are beyond the powers of a scryer" he said, " I can tell you bring certain powers to me today, as strong as you bring the gods from the north."

"You are pretty good yourself, just dial it down a little, you don't have to impress me, " said Christina, although she was already wondering about how he got to gods from the north.

He sounded relieved, " Okay, I wasn't expecting anyone for about half an hour."

"Okay, that's not the best of fortune teller explanations, " smiled Christina, " So what do you prefer as a personal pronoun?"

At this the teller recovered slightly, " You know something, I hardly ever get asked, but as you have, let me say I don't really mind. When I'm looking feminine, the 'she' is good, when I'm masculine, then 'he' works for me, but when I'm in here, I can handle 'they' as well."

Christina laughed, " I'm from Iceland, where we have masculine, feminine and neuter. You can normally tell which is the right one to use."

"So, you are saying I'm an exception?" asked the fortune teller.

"I expect you are an exception to many rules, " laughed Christina, " So you'll have to tell me your name, I'm Christina."

"I'm Roberta, " answered the fortune teller, " I like you."

"That's good. Let me cross your palm with some silver."

"A credit card is also good, " replied Roberta.

"Okay, then, let me tell you want I'm interested in first. I just need some ideas."

"Go on, " said Roberta, " I think you've done this kind of thing before."

"My mother was a Chinese trapeze artist, " answered Christina.

"Ha ha, " said Roberta, " In pre-war Paris, Smuggling bombs for the underground."

"Very good, " said Christina, " You know them too, "

"The Decemberists? I sometimes sing one of their songs in my stage act- on the uke, but not that one. But you know something, I can tell, someone in your line has been a Russian cadet in your past."

Christina felt as if something small had just walked across her back. How could this guy possibly know she had been a Russian Cadet in Arkhangelsk?

"Now you are starting to intrigue me, " she said.

"My friend phoned me, she wants me to look into a company called Raven."

"Raven, " said Roberta, " You know that is a powerful symbol."

"Many references to ravens exist in world lore and literature. Because of its black plumage, croaking call and diet of carrion, the raven is often associated with loss and ill omen.

"Yet a raven's symbolism is complex. As a talking bird, the raven also represents prophecy and insight. Ravens in stories often connect the material world with the world of spirits.

"What? Like psychopomps?" asked Christina.

"Christina, who are you?" asked Roberta looking surprised, " to know of psychopomps?

"Those are the guides through the various transitions of life. Like from Greek *pompos* (conductor or guide) and *psyche* (breath, life, soul, or mind). Stories of psychopomps are widespread throughout the mythological tales, religious texts, sacred narratives, and real-life stories of people around the world."

"My strange education, I suppose, I was brought up living in different countries."

"Well, some of the most well-known psychopomps include the Greek god Hermes, the Egyptian jackal-headed god Anubis, the Archangel Michael, and the female Valkyries of Teutonic legend. A wide variety of angels, animals, birds, and other helpful beings have also been known to act as guides to the afterlife. And Archangels too, in general."

"Well, let's just say I have a special relationship with Archangel Michael. But don't go all seance-y on me. I'm much more interested in Ravens and anything about something called Brant."

"Brant - like brannt or verbrannt, " said Roberta, " Burning or burnt"

"Go back to ravens, " said Christina.

"I will, " said Roberta, " but first you remind me of something important."

"Das Narrenshiff. The Ship of Fools. I believe the first to use the phrase 'Ship of Fools' was Sebastian Brant, back in the 1400s. Ship of Fools: a ship—an entire fleet at first—sets off from Basel, bound for the Paradise of Fools. In it, Brant conceives Saint Grobian, whom he imagines to be the patron saint of vulgar and coarse people."

Roberta continued, " You know the story? It goes right back to Plato. The ship of fools is an allegory, originating from Plato's Republic, about a ship with a dysfunctional crew.

"The allegory is intended to represent the problems of governance prevailing in a political system not based on expert knowledge, such as democracies."

"This is interesting, " said Christina, there was still a chill in her back.

Roberta continued, " Well, there's the shipowner, larger and stronger than everyone in the ship, but somewhat deaf and rather short-sighted, with a knowledge of sailing to match his eyesight.

He leaned forward and softened his voice, " The sailors are quarrelling among themselves over captaincy of the ship, each one thinking he ought to be captain, though he has never learnt that skill, nor can he point to the person who taught him or a time when he was learning it. On top of which they say it can't be taught. In fact, they're prepared to cut to pieces anyone who says it can. The shipowner himself is always surrounded by them.

"They beg him and do everything they can to make him hand over the tiller to them.

"Then they immobilise their worthy shipowner with drugs or drink or by some other means, and take control of the ship, helping themselves to what it is carrying.

"Drinking and feasting, they sail in the way you'd expect people like that to sail.

"As for how the captain will steer the ship - regardless of whether anyone wants him to - they do not regard this as an additional skill or study which can be acquired over and above the art of being a ship's captain. "

Roberta paused, then asked, " If this is the situation on board, don't you think the person who is genuinely equipped to be captain will be called a stargazer, a chatterer, of no use to them, by those who sail in ships with this kind of crew?

"Fascinating, " said Christina, " But I think I should pay you now. You said someone else arrives here around now."

"No, not really, " said Roberta, " I always say something like that to my guests, to make them think I am in demand. If I have a difficult customer, I also know that they can go after half an hour. See, I'm giving you my trade secrets now."

"Like running an air conditioner behind me to make me feel the chills?" asked Christina.

"Okay, you got me, " said Roberta, " But I said already that I liked you. What are you, Russian born? I don't think so. But you've travelled a lot.

"Back to the raven. If you've a Russian background, you'll associate the raven with death or more specifically with an aftermath of a bloody or significant battle. Ravens often appear in pairs and play the role of harbingers of tragic news, usually announcing death of a hero or a group of heroes.

"But in other indigenous cultures, like the Native American Indians and even as far as the Inuits and Iceland the raven is the Creator of the world, but it is also considered a trickster god.

"What, like Loki?"

"Like Loki in the Viking stories, not the Marvel movies. By the time Tom Hiddleston took over, it had been somewhat corrupted."

"But let's take the Russian view for a moment, in Russian Pacific north-west Tlingit culture, there are two distinct raven characters which can be identified, although they are not always clearly differentiated.

"One is the creator raven, responsible for bringing the

world into being and who is sometimes considered to be the individual who brought light to the darkness. The other is the childish raven, always selfish, sly, conniving, and hungry.

"When the Great Spirit created all things, he kept them separate and stored in cedar boxes. The Great Spirit gifted these boxes to the animals who existed before humans.

"When the animals opened the boxes all the things that comprise the world came into being. The boxes held such things as mountains, fire, water, wind and seeds for all the plants.

"If you hear the Navajo native Americans tell this story, they will tell it a different way, with a fox that caught the sun in its mouth, but it is all stories with the same ideas.

"So, one such box held by the animals was given to Seagull and contained all the light of the world. Seagull coveted his box and refused to open it, clutching it under his wing. All the people asked Raven to persuade Seagull to open it and release the light. Despite begging, demanding, flattering and trying to trick him into opening the box, Seagull still refused.

"Finally Raven became angry and frustrated and stuck a thorn in Seagull's foot. Raven pushed the thorn in deeper until the pain caused Seagull to drop the box. Then out of the box came the sun, moon and stars that brought light to the world and allowed the first day to begin."

"Wow, " said Christina, " Thank you, and how did you know all of that?"

"Honestly? I act as well as doing this. I was in a show at

Theatre 503 about the Ship of Fools and another one about Native American people, it's amazing how much I can work in from my other roles."

Christina smiled again; she'd got plenty of stimulating ideas to take into the assignment suggested by Elena.

"Here's my card, " she said, " You can probably predict how much I will pay."

Roberta smiled, " Here's my flyer for my next show, it's in the Vaults, by Waterloo. I'll be doing a cabaret sketch show. Dress wild. Sorry - I mean dress even wilder."

"I'll try to be there, " smiled Christina.

Put us in the corner 'cause we're into ideas

Christina left Roberta's fortune telling shop in the Box Park. She would have to hurry across to where she said she'd meet the others.

"Hi, Christina, " called a voice.

Christina turned around, " We're over here."

She hurried over to a table. There, in a corner, sat Clare and Bigsy.

Clare was looking a little preoccupied on a phone call.

"It'll only be a minute, " she mouthed.

Bigsy stood and shook Christina's hand.

"Hi Bigsy, how's it going?" asked Christina.

"It's going good, " said Bigsy, " I've finished the studio, you know, you're welcome to try it any time."

"Thanks, Bigsy, but I still need a low profile, " answered Christina, " I was just called up by my friend from

Amsterdam, actually, "

Bigsy had a sizeable burger in front of him, " Have a French fry, " he offered, " They are delish."

"I'm good, " said Christina. Clare pressed her phone off, and leapt up to hug Christina, " How are you - I thought you were camped out in Amsterdam nowadays?" asked Clare.

"I've made a return to London, " answered Christina, " And there's an assignment in it as well - for The Triangle, if you like."

"It's a case of straight fees and then a risk and reward tail to it."

Clare looked intrigued, " But I thought you'd checked out from the Life?"

"Checked out, checked back in, " said Christina, " Wait until you hear about my little puzzle."

Christina recounted the story of Raven and how they were hiving off a part of the company into Brant Holdings. That the new part was being filled with the unwanted people from the old organisation - just like in the old story of the Ship of Fools.

"That's okay, " said Clare, " But what's the angle on it?"

"Why are they doing it?" added Bigsy.

"It can't just be for money, can it?" asked Clare.

"No, there's got to be a higher stake. Maybe state manipulation, " agreed Christina.

"Now I've got a tricky question for you, " said Clare, looking at Christina.

"I know you changed your name and went into almost exile after your last exploit with us. You said it was something to do with Chuck Manners. Well, Chuck is back on the scene. He is with Jake right now. He's over from America and asked to see Jake. What would happen if he met you?" Clare looked at Christina.

"Do you know, I've really got no idea, " said Christina, " I've changed my name, stopped producing any kind of music to throw people from the trail and was hoping that there wouldn't be anyone following me."

"Well, Chuck has had to do that a few times, " said Bigsy, " Remember when he had to lie low after that van explosion in London? - You remember - the one outside the Bank of England?"

Christina nodded, " Yes, I'm just not sure how he would react to my reappearance now."

"Well, let's be honest, there's more to you than we ever realised, " said Clare, " I think you've got a few secrets tucked away somewhere?"

Christina nodded, " For another time maybe."

Getting a grip

Christina called Elena again.

"Hi Elena, I've been following up on your situation."

"Christina, that's great. It looks as if we are being divested in the next stage. The Brussels office will remain but we, from the Amsterdam office, are to go to Brant."

"Do you know the timescales?" asked Christina.

"It's best to ask Nelson about all of that, " said Elena, " He seems better connected to the big picture than we are in the Dutch office. Also, he's based in London, so you should find it easy enough to see him.

"He says there's a reward now for figuring this out. It's in shares though. A lot of Raven shares which would transfer across to you. He's involved with a consortium of agitated shareholders."

"Okay, I'll go visit him, but you'd better tell him I'll be along, " said Christina.

"Sure thing, " said Elena.

A few days later Christina received an email from Nelson. He asked to meet Christina at the Head Office of Raven, in London. Christina confirmed the arrangement and then contacted Clare to provide some additional cover during the meeting.

Raven

Christina, Clare and Bigsy all arrived in separate cabs at the offices Nelson had specified. The offices of Raven were not what they had expected. They expected a tall, plate glass building, but arrived at what looked like a stone building from the early 20th century.

"This doesn't look much like a Corporate Headquarters, " said Clare, " I hope we have come to the right place."

"It is probably like a lot of august organisations in central London, they keep their older buildings for show and then build big operations centres in places like Canary Wharf, " suggested Bigsy.

"The old Lloyds Bank board room used to be close to the Bank of England, then the building got turned into a fancy pub, nowadays it is gym, " said Clare, " and along the road from it, there's that old bank vault which has been made into a cocktail bar."

"Yes, and there's that oil company in St James, that looks like it is in quite a small building, but that's because they have all their operations centres around the outskirts of London, " added Bigsy.

They entered the Raven building, through heavy doors and were greeted with a neat looking reception desk, off to one side of the main lobby. A couple of low-key security people stood around the entrance area. Bigsy could see a few black leather sofas along the edge of what was an ornate entrance hall.

Clare was looking at the diagonal black-and-white tiled flooring, " It's Masonic, " she whispered, " Their head office is an old Masonic Hall - look up"

She pointed to the vaulted ceiling. It was breathtakingly decorated with stars and constellations, " That will be the stars at a particular point in time, " she said, " like when this building was built or when the Grand Lodge of England formed - it's to remind Masons that everyone lives under the same sky."

"How do you know so much about this?" asked Bigsy.

"My father was a mason until he gave it up, and he used to take us to an open-air museum, where they had rebuilt a whole temple. The guys that ran it used to tell us the stories, " she replied.

"But I thought it was all secret?" asked Bigsy.

"Except the bits that are not secret, " said Clare and winked.

"So will Nelson give us a dodgy handshake?" asked Bigsy, " You know, all fingers and thumbs?"

"I don't know about that, " said Clare, " you have to count along the knuckles to know which degree of mason you're dealing with in their handshake. But remember the Masons are a bit weird about women. They had to set up separate societies for women members. The main lodges are still men only."

"And look, there's a sunburst in the centre of the ceiling. You can tell where the Master sits, in the east, by a rising star above his chair and then a setting sun in the west above the Senior Warden's chair."

"What about the 'G' in the middle there?" Asked Bigsy, is that for God or something?

"Not quite, " said Clare, " I think it stands for Great Architect, I suppose, a Supreme Being believed in by all Freemasons. My father said the later versions of the Masons pinched a lot from Christianity to drop into their symbols. It is like the clean-up of Pagan ways conducted by the Church by marking everything with crosses.

"Yes, " said Bigsy, " I remember, like the original meaning of hot cross buns was the wheel of life, in Pagan times – grand scale re-purposing"

"I've seen that serpent eating its own tail somewhere else, " said Christina pointing to a circular depiction, " Ouroboros - alchemy - I think it is a symbol for infinity."

"Yes, the circle of life, " said Clare, miming holding out a lion cub, like the Disney movie.

"But what about the seven stars inside of it?" asked Bigsy,

"I think there's a giveaway on the walls, answered Christina, " Look: grammar, rhetoric, logic, arithmetic, geometry, music and astronomy."

Christina noticed some brochures on the reception counter.

"Look, " she said, " This leaflet is all about the hall!"

She picked it up and read about the hall decoration,

"Look, it says here that The Master's symbol is the square, said to be the controlling force. The Junior Warden represents the sun, marking it at its highest point and seated on the south side. The plumb rule is his symbol of justness and upright behaviour.

" The Senior Warden, represented by the moon after sunset, sits opposite the Master in the west, from where he attends to the closing of the lodge. His symbol is the level showing equality.

"The candlesticks also represent the roles played by the three men using the three main orders of architecture: Ionic, Doric and Corinthian. The Master's is of the Ionic order denoting wisdom; the Senior Warden's is of the Doric order denoting strength, and that by the Junior Warden of the Corinthian order denotes beauty."

"Okay, well I think we can safely say that we are in the zone now, " said Bigsy, " Except that it might not allow you two ladies to go much further."

At that moment Nelson appeared. They had expected him to come from somewhere inside of the building, but he arrived at the same front door that they had walked through.

"Nelson?" asked Christina.

"That's right, " he answered, " You must be the friend of

Elena - Christina isn't it? she spoke very highly of you."

Hi, and we are two colleagues of Christina, " said Bigsy, self-consciously shaking hands with Nelson.

"I'm Bigsy and this is Clare, " Clare smiled at Nelson.

"This is one mighty impressive place you've got for a headquarters, " said Bigsy.

"Yes, I wanted to show it to you, I'm normally based in the Corporate Operations building in Canary Wharf, " said Nelson, " But let's have a brief look around here and then we can go grab a coffee or something outside."

He looked around and all three of them realised that this might not be the best place to talk.

"So, what actually happened here, then?" asked Bigsy.

"Sure, " said Nelson, " I know - I'll ask the receptionist to find us one of the guides."

They spent the next half hour walking around to the various rooms, while the guide from Raven gave them a brief corporate history.

At the end, Bigsy asked Nelson, " So okay, Are you one?"

Clare and Christina looked over at Nelson.

"There's a little clause about no bondsmen, which doesn't seem to have been revoked around here, " said Nelson.

"Bondsmen, what the slave trade?" asked Bigsy.

"Yes, " said Nelson, " You'll probably have deduced I'm

of Caribbean descent!"

"Of course, " said Bigsy, " What was I thinking!"

"No, you are right to question it all nowadays, " said Nelson, " The Masons project outwardly that they have no race or creed issues. That they are open to anyone. That all you need to do is be a man and believe in a Higher Being. That the Masons are not secretive and don't do favours for one another."

"That's a mighty good piece of PR, " said Clare, " My father said there were all kinds of secrets and initiations. He did it for a while, but said he got tired of the whole thing. It wasn't compatible with his line of work either, which involved driving. Most of the members seemed to drink a little too frequently to routinely hold a steering wheel."

"Speaking of which, shall we go across to the pub, then?" suggested Bigsy, " It'll be easier to talk there."

"That was my thinking too, " said Nelson, " Maybe not the Freemason's Arm's though - which is just around the corner."

"How about that Irish place, " suggested Clare, " Philomena's? They do food too, I think."

"Good idea, " said Nelson, " Although I should point out it is right by the side of Freemason's Hall, "

"Are we in the Masonic part of London, by any chance?" asked Christina.

"You could say that, " answered Nelson.

Philomena's

Christina was relieved to see the Philomena's was an Irish style bar. There was sport showing on the televisions, but it looked as if it was old football matches being replayed.

They sat together, Bigsy brought over a tray of drinks, which included a couple of Guinness. Nelson called up a friend to join them, " He's called Javel Blackwood - he's an analyst whizz."

"It's a bit like a school classroom in here, " said Bigsy, " and if we are going to talk about, " he lowered his voice, " ahem freemasons, then I think we might need to go somewhere different."

Clare looked around. The next table had four slightly drunk looking businessmen seated at it. Across the way was another group of five, suited and booted talking loudly about some kind of deal they were trying to win.

They kept referring to "the client" but Clare thought she had worked out who it was, by their references to St.

James and 'petro-chem'. The youngest looking of them looked freshly kitted out and his bags were all neatly displaying their firm's name.

"I'd be somewhat horrified to hear the consultants talking about my organisation like that, " she said, " especially as we can see who they are, too."

"It's the way things work now, " said Nelson, " Bring in the hired guns to provide sanctions in line with whatever the man or woman at the top wants."

Clare could also see that they would be overheard in this pub.

"We need to move again, " she said.

Christina nodded, " I agree, and - don't all look around - but I think that guy with the green over jacket followed us in here. We'll see if he follows us to the next place."

Bigsy finished his beer. A particularly fine glass of Guinness. He looked at the person that Christina had identified. Forty-ish, weathered skin, quietly sipping a cola, and sitting at the bar.

"Let's go then, " he announced.

"What about Nelson's friend?" asked Christina.

"Javel? - I'll text him with the change of plan. Where are we going?"

"Indian, " said Bigsy, " We'll find somewhere."

The others followed him, and they all set off toward Long Acre and towards the bustle of Covent Garden.

A few minutes later they had found a place in Floral Street.

"Perfect, we'll get a table and Nelson can tell us all about what has been happening to Raven."

Nelson was busily texting to Javel.

"And don't look now, but our friend has followed us here, " said Clare. Christina also looked up.

"Do you want him gone?" she asked.

"No let's observe, " said Clare, " It might be useful to know some more."

Sfogliatelle

They looked at the menu. Bigsy had done well, and they now had a compressive selection of Indian food to select from.

"Poppadoms, " announced Bigsy, " While we wait for Javel."

At that moment Nelson stood up.

"Hey Javel, you found us then!"

Javel smiled, round-faced, close cut dark hair, a small beard under the chin and a vibrant green shirt underneath a suit jacket. The merest hint of a beaded necklace.

"Hey Nelson, Hello friends, Nelson has been leading me a merry dance around London."

"How did you get here?" asked Clare.

"Aw, all right then, Nelson was leading the taxi-driver a merry dance."

"You over from CW?" asked Nelson.

"Yes, what are you doing so close to Head Office?" asked Javel.

"I wanted to tell these people something about what has been happening over at Raven."

"Ah yes, Raven spins off Brant, Board Members in line for huge bonuses!" said Javel, " I can predict the headlines now."

"Okay Javel, I think you can explain about Raven's business exploits better than me."

Javel began, " Okay, let's start at the beginning. Raven was founded in 1920 and is one of the world's largest providers of products and services to the energy industry.

"Raven employs over 60,000 people in over 80 countries. It claims to maximise value through the lifetime of the energy reservoir. Then it has spun off a whole raft of other interests. Once it is operating at near scale in a country, it invests and develops the infrastructure too.

"A few example countries outside of the USA or UK where Raven operates are Venezuela, Saudi Arabia, Canada, Iran, Iraq, Kuwait, the UAE, Libya and Nigeria.

"Most of them are unstable. Venezuela has two competing Presidents; President Maduro, who had been sworn in to a second six-year term in office and acting president Mr Guaidó trying to get the military to switch their allegiance to him.

Javel continued, " Saudi Arabia is mostly thought of as a totalitarian absolute monarchy with Islamist lines, where the King is both the head of state and government. US airbases to give the US reach into the middle east."

"Yes, and I get it that Iran, Iraq, Libya are all in turmoil and with heavy US presence, both seen and unseen, " said Jake.

Javel continued, " Kuwait - Like a key block in a board game - a desert stuck in the corner between Saudi and Iraq. The US treats it as a partner now, after the conflicts of Desert Shield and Desert Storm. It has sold Kuwait a large number of 'defensive' missiles and airborne defences too."

Javel paused and looked around, " You get the picture, without me carrying on. Raven operates in all of these territories. And it is no secret that there's been revolving doors between big business and government. "

"It's another case of the 'Stupid White Men' who run big business, said Nelson, " Except they are not so stupid, "

Javel continued, " I can't prove anything, but I think there's been some kind of lobbying running."

"The Americans fight a war somewhere and blow up a place. Then it is time for a large infrastructure corporation to come in and repair it."

Nelson agreed, " That's been Raven's business model for ages. Okay, it builds hospitals and shopping malls too, but most of its non-energy income is from what I guess you'd call war reparations."

Javel added darkly, " It's not unlike the crows that descended on battlefields in medieval times, only the picking here are millions of dollars.

"With supplying the fuel, helping build military bases, supplying the war machine, conducting the clean-up and extending the infrastructure, one could call it a virtuous business cycle" added Javel, " The share price has done well out of it, as have the main board.

"In the US, the Pentagon's Defense Policy Board has connections with highly paid consultants for companies hoping to profit from conflicts."

"It's all a matter of cashflow. How many days can the US run a bombardment and how much revenue generation will it create as a consequence?" said Javel.

"That's sick, isn't it?" asked Clare.

"Well it's definitely immoral, profiteering from a war, " answered Nelson.

"So, you are saying that Raven has interests in this form of business?" asked Christina, " No wonder you wanted to talk about it away from the Head Office."

Javel said, " Well, let's just look back for a moment at a few encounters.

He started, " There's Libya. The second Libyan Civil War, which has seen the US deploy hundreds of airstrikes against the Islamic State. The cheque might be in the post on that one.

After a pause, Javel added, " Then there's Yemen. A War

on Terror target and part of the ISIS Campaign. The US put a naval blockade in as well as supporting Saudi Arabia to bomb large chunks of the territory. And let's not forget that Yemen is one of the poorest countries on the planet, beset with famine and cholera. That all kicked off in 2015 and is still running."

"Yes, I see that footage of the poor people and wonder how they can afford to run such wars., " said Clare.

Javel continued, " How about Syria? It's part of Operation Inherent Resolve, the Syrian Civil War, the War on Terror and the International ISIS campaign, so it has around 20 forces involved now. The US alone is estimated to have run over 11,000 airstrikes into Syria. That all started in 2014."

"I suppose giving it a mission name like that helps to legitimise it?" asked Clare.

Javel nodded, " Take Iraq - another example? It is another part of Operation Inherent Resolve, the Iraqi Civil War, the spill over of the Syrian Civil War, the War on Terror and the International ISIS campaign. Another dozen or more countries involved, including troops from Australia, New Zealand and Canada. This one tallies over 13,000 airstrikes into the zone."

Nelson chipped in, " The same thing with Operation Ocean Shield, which was the Indian Ocean pirate ship reduction, also put down to the War on Terror."

Javel continued, " So like Clare says, the US will adopt an attitudinal position branded with a campaign, like 'Ocean Shield, Desert Storm, Inherent Resolve, The War on Terror' and then drop troops and armament to smash up the landscape. After the designated number of days, it'll declare victory and bring in the cavalry to tidy things up."

"...Were you ever beaten up at school?" asked Bigsy, " and then had the bully's henchmen tidy you up again afterwards?"

"That's a kind of Mafia trick, " said Christina, " Sfogliatelle; where they rough someone up, then shove a lovely pastry in their mouth. It's like a warning."

"Where'd you learn that stuff?" asked Bigsy. Christina looked at Clare.

"Oh, in my travels, " said Christina.

"I always knew you were bad-ass, " said Bigsy.

"More than you might realise, " answered Christina, smiling.

"Are you two flirting?" asked Nelson.

"No, " answered Christina still smiling.

Bigsy could feel his face redden.

"So, what have we got then?" asked Clare, " A tricksy organisation which seems to be profiteering on the back of US-declared wars?"

"Yes, " agreed Nelson, " And of course it isn't the only one. There are many friends of people in high places who dip their noses in the trough from time to time."

"But do you think something new is about to happens? Based upon the company spin-off?"

Nelson leaned forward, " Well, think about it. Raven is, at heart, an energy company. They exploit energy globally. Find it, extract it, refine it, ship it, trade it."

Javel also leaned it, " And now we are joining the dots. Oil has always been a primitive leading cause of war - and Raven has seen its share of them. Political effects generated by the oil industry makes oil a driver towards war. At least a quarter and maybe as much as one-half of wars since 1973 have been connected to oil-related causes."

Nelson added, " No other commodity has had such an impact on international security and in a country like the US the influence of oil on conflict is often poorly understood."

Javel nodded, " America will usually find other public debate to deflect from their economic interest. In the 1991 and 2003 Iraq wars, both sides focused excessively on the question of whether the United States was fighting for possession of oil reserves; neither sought a broader understanding of how oil shaped the preconditions for war."

"Remember how the Americans were told by President Bush and his administration that the U.S. was going to war with Iraq because of the imminent threat of Saddam's weapons of mass destruction and ties to terrorism?

"Oh yes, they never found any WMDs, " said Bigsy.

"Exactly, " said Javel, " Look I'm sorry if I sound too polarised about this, but I'm really trying to stick to facts."

Javel continued, " Then another justification for invasion was the purported link between Saddam Hussein's government and terrorist organizations, in particular Al-Qaeda.

"I'm not saying that Saddam wasn't a tyrant, but the cause was branded so wide as to allow all kinds of other American actions.

"In that sense, the Bush Administration cast the Iraq war as part of the broader War on Terrorism. Remember, in 2013, FBI Director Robert Mueller testified to Congress that 'seven countries designated as State Sponsors of Terrorism—Iran, Iraq, Syria, Sudan, Libya, Cuba, and North Korea—remain active in the US and continue to support terrorist groups that have targeted Americans.'

"Well, that brought out the overarching branding of 'War on Terror' - used in several subsequent and ongoing conflicts, and the oil situation goes as an unnoticed third or fourth agenda topic.

"A bit like 'God on our side arguments,' " said Bigsy.

"Hmm. Yes and no, the religious zealots have stayed out of a lot of this. It has been a more secular set of claims that drive the US branding of campaigns. Remember USA is multi-cultured, so a religious backdrop would only get factional."

"So, as with the argument that Iraq was developing biological and nuclear weapons, evidence linking Saddam Hussein and Al-Qaeda was discredited by multiple U.S. intelligence agencies soon after the invasion of Iraq."

"It is well-known that critics of the Bush administration say in the build-up to war with Iraq, policy-makers were cherry-picking intelligence from CIA and other intelligence agencies, publicising only the information that would bolster the case for war and ignoring contrary evidence."

"Yes, it was a big deal here in the UK too, with Blair portrayed as a poodle to Bush. Massive protests and a disputed report. A scientist involved in the report committed suicide, " said Bigsy.

It wasn't really in the interest of politicians to do otherwise than to spin it all. Sure, they couldn't help stem the footage of oilfields on fire, but there was still spin about fighting for the freedom of the people and similar stories.

"But why would this current situation require a divestment?" asked Clare, " Surely Raven must be impenetrable by now?"

"Yes, that's what we thought, " answered Javel, " They have enough people in high places to be unassailable."

"That's unless there's a new situation about to go down," said Javel, " New lobbying, maybe a new country about to be put in the searchlights?"

"How will we find out?" asked Bigsy.

"Dib, dib, dib, " said Clare.

"What, you think there's a Masonic twist in this?" asked Bigsy.

"Hello!" said Clare sarcastically, " Top Masons run a

company which trades into conflict zones. Maybe has some links to the UK government? It might be spmething else, but the evidence is starting to stack up. It does raise the question about how we'd ever get a look though."

Christina stood.

"I'll just be a minute, " she said as she walked towards the ladies' room.

"So how long have you two known one another?" asked Clare, looking at both Nelson and Javel.

"Pretty much since I worked for Raven, " said Nelson. "I ran into Javel in the first week. We were at a company offsite and I didn't know so many people. I'd just gone back to the bar and Javel was standing there with a laptop. I made some quip about working too hard and he came back with a remark about needing it finished so that the share price would go up.

"I believed him, of course, not that he was just answering an email from his daughter."

"We've been buddies since that time in Brussels, " replied Javel, " And strange as it may seem, we work in the same building yet normally only see one another in the canteen or when we are at an off-site."

"Not at all, " said Clare, " I believe you - It's the modern way, what with virtualised meetings and ATCs all the time."

"Yes, " agreed Bigsy, at least with an Audio Tele Conference I can be doing something else while I listen to the over-lengthy messages from the big chiefs."

There was a crash.

They all looked around. It was Christina, she had just stumbled on the bag of the man who she thought had been following them.

"I'm so sorry, " she was saying, the man looked embarrassed as he stood to wipe wine from his shirt.

"It's okay, " he said, " It was my fault to leave the bag there."

"I think I tripped on its carry strap, " said Christina, " I always have to watch out if I'm carrying a bag like that."

A waiter had appeared and was ushering Christina back to her seat. Another waiter was checking that the man was okay.

"Oops, Sfogliatelle " said Christina, as she sat down. Clare looked her. She had done something.

"At this rate we will need to move to yet another bar!" said Bigsy.

"Then we would need to reclassify the evening as a pub crawl, " answered Clare, " I'm sorry guys, " she said looking towards Nelson and Javel, " We can't take Christina anywhere!"

# The Triangle

"heart, mind and desire"

Christina Hyde

They had left the Indian Restaurant.

"How will we keep in contact?" asked Nelson.

"Don't worry about that, " said Clare, " I'll be in contact over the next couple of days. We need to do some digging first. You and Lieke were right, there's something very fishy about all of this."

They split up, and Nelson and Javel grabbed a cab.

"Let's walk, " said Christina, the others nodded.

"So, what do we think?" asked Clare, " It looks like a business model to get work on the back of war damages."

"Yes, but that doesn't explain why they would want to hive off to Brant Holdings though, " said Bigsy.

Christina looked around, " The guy. The one following us, He's gone now. I saw him get in a cab after the others."

"Is he following them?" Asked Bigsy.

"Could be, but if he is then its Nelson who is being tailed. I wonder why?" said Christina.

"Perhaps this will help us to find out?" she held out a phone.

"No way!" said Clare, " You didn't steal that from him!"

"Borrow, " said Christina, " Borrow. We'll return it later."

"To where though?"

"Maybe to his home address. On the way into the ladies' room I borrowed his wallet. I've taken photographs of its content, which included his driving licence. It will be quite disturbing to him when we send the phone through the post. Don't worry I put his wallet back in his jacket."

"What about *where_is_my_phone.com*?" asked Bigsy, looking worried.

"I think we can lose the phone fast, once we have copied its memory, " said Christina.

"How will we get past the pin number?" asked Bigsy.

"Well, the excellent news is that he's left it as four digits, " said Christina, " And it's an iPhone, so we can't use 4 digits the same."

"Okay, " said Bigsy. "Give me a moment. Excluding repeats, the most common pins are: 1234 1212 1004 2000 6969 1122 1313 4321 2001 1010." Normally I'd include 1111, 2222 etc. but on an iPhone that won't work."

"He looked more like a minimum movement kind of guy to me, " said Christina, " Clandestine, so he needs to work the phone when it is still in his pocket."

"1212 or 1414, " she announced, " I know it is not on your list, Bigsy, but it is an easy one to feel for using the edge of the phone."

They all watched as she typed in "1414." To their amazement, it worked.

"We're in, " she said as she flicked across to the security settings and removed a couple.

"Er, where did you learn all of this?" asked Bigsy, slightly startled to see Christina so proficient at phone hacking.

"Basic skills training, " answered Christina.

"What, at music school?" answered Bigsy.

"Not exactly, " said Christina, " I should tell Bigsy?" she looked towards Clare.

"Yes, " said Clare, " I know Bigsy will be discreet."

Okay, said Christina, " Bigsy, I don't want to freak you out, but I'm not quite what you thought I was."

"What, a lovely pop-star that I know?" answered Bigsy.

"There's more, " answered Christina, " I'm also a trained agent."

"What? Microsoft software engineer? Carphone Warehouse agent?" asked Bigsy.

"No, you are being silly. I'm an agent for a foreign government - or I was, anyway."

"What Holland, or -wait - America?" asked Bigsy.

"Not quite, " said Christina, " I have worked for the Russian government."

Bigsy looked at Clare to see if she was grinning. He could not work out her expression.

"I was trained in Russia and have then worked in many countries. Nowadays I'm resting."

Bigsy looked incredulous. "Em, this is quite a lot to take in. Does Clare know this already? What about Jake?"

Clare answered, " Christina told me about this some time ago. She swore me to secrecy, although I've really wanted to tell both of you about this."

"You'd be such an asset to us in the Triangle, " said Bigsy, excited that they were with a Russian agent.

"But wait, are you rearranging all of our election results and manipulating events through twitter and social media?" he asked.

"No, " said Christina, " Although I have visited a click-farm."

"Really, " said Bigsy, " I've always wanted to see how they worked...Are they hot inside, with all of that technology?"

"Let's leave it that I've been trained by the FSB to do a lot of stuff, and I still know how to do it."

"FSB? Is that like the KGB?" asked Bigsy.

"Bigsy, it is the KGB - Don't you remember they were renamed?" said Clare.

"Wow, Christina Nott, KGB Agent, " said Bigsy.

"Not quite...Christina Hyde, FSB Agent, " replied Christina.

"I see - we used to make jokes about you being Nott Christina, and now you are Hyde-ing?" smiled Bigsy.

Then as if as an afterthought, " Whoa, so Christina - did you get married - hence the Hyde?"

"No Bigsy, I'm still single, if you are asking. My name change is in the interests of my profession."

Clare laughed.

Clone a phone

They looked back to the phone.

Maybe this would yield something.

"We should get this back to my place, " said Bigsy, " That way we can clone it and download a copy of all the data."

Christina persisted to check around the phone. She tapped phone album. There were several pictures of them all sitting in the restaurant. He had propped the phone up on the table to take these. Christina had come over during the photo sessions. It was why it had been so easy to lift the phone.

Next she tried the email. It was almost empty. There were a couple of emails to another anonymous google mail user id. It was just a number series.

"Old-school number code, " said Christina, " and not Russian."

They took a taxi back to Bigsy's place. He had moved to an apartment block in East London, close to Canary Wharf.

"It's easy for me to get to where my clients are, from here, " he explained, " Most of them are one or two stops away, or even walking. I've figured out the subterranean world of Canary Wharf and can usually walk in a straight line to wherever I need to be."

"It's a lovely place, " said Christina, looking around the flat, " How many bedrooms? It looks pretty spacious."

"Yes, two beds, although I've kitted the second one out as a kind of office, " said Bigsy, " Take a look."

He showed them in, although it surprised neither Clare nor Christina to see it was full of technology and bookshelves.

"Neat!" said Clare, who was used to Bigsy's sense of order. "And will some of that stuff let us copy that iPhone?"

Bigsy retrieved the phone from his pocket. Christina noticed it was also in a little pouch.

"What's that? A shield?" asked Christina.

"Yes, " said Bigsy. I was concerned about it being able to track us on this journey, so I shielded it. I'll do the same when we connect it up. I got the shield from a Madonna gig. They were stopping us from making recordings or taking photos."

He went to a wardrobe with sliding doors. He looked to the floor and riffled through some flat objects.

"This one, " he said, as he finally picked a laptop from the pile, " I know, some people have shoe collections. Oh, I nearly forgot. Would you ladies like a drink?"

"We'll help ourselves while you set up the wizardry, " said Clare, leading Christina back into the kitchen area.

Bigsy busied himself with wires and connections, before also returning to the kitchen.

"I'm copying everything from the phone to the laptop, " he said, " The iPhone thinks the laptop is another iPhone, and it is doing what normally happens when you buy a new phone and want to make a copy of your old one to it."

"Excellent, " said Clare, " So we can still read it from the laptop?"

"Yes, or we could even make another identical phone, " said Bigsy.

"When we've finished, we should put it back in the pouch, but ultimately post it back to its owner. If we do that anonymously, he might even think it was an accident or that he lost it."

"Agreed, " said Bigsy, " How about adding an anonymous message, like "found in the street."

"No, said Christina, " We should just let him wonder."

Bigsy checked the progress of his copying.

"It's finished, " he said, " Successful."

"Okay, are you all right to dispose of the phone?" asked Clare.

"Yes, you bet, " said Bigsy, " Let's see what we've got."

Burner

Together they huddled around the screen. Bigsy had done well, and they seemed to have everything faithfully copied from the phone. There was not a lot of information.

"What can we tell?" asked Clare.

"It looks like a one-purpose phone...A burner, " said Bigsy, " Like the kind that drug dealers use."

"Except this is being used for something else?" asked Christina.

"Yes, and that's probably why there is only one number stored on it. Probably a control, " said Bigsy.

"What are the language settings?" asked Christina, " And have they ever been changed?"

"Ah yes, interesting, it is set to English - American English though, and look, it has been set to Russian at some point."

"Photos?" asked Christina.

"Only the ones in the Indian Restaurant, " said Bigsy.

"Try the camera, " asked Christina.

"Ah yes, there's something else there. A couple of snaps of a document, " said Bigsy, " It's in Russian."

"Let me look, " asked Christina.

"She paused and then translated, " It's about oil…

"Russian Arctic: So far this year, Russia has discovered nearly 1.5 billion barrels of oil equivalent (Bboe) thanks to the Dinkov and Nyarmeyskoye finds on the Yamal peninsula shelf in the Kara Sea. In natural gas terms, that's 17 trillion cubic feet (Tcf).

"When it comes to Arctic oil, Russia's state-run firm is having a tougher time. To get its Arctic projects off the ground, the state-run company will need $40 billion in tax cuts from the government.

"According to The Moscow Times, the state-run oil company has secured a deal with Indian financiers to invest in a 15 to 20-percent stake, but that would only happen if the state-run company was granted a $40-billion tax break over the next 30 years.

The problem for investors is that while the Vostok Oil project reserves are worth around $15 billion, climate change is causing oil and gas infrastructure to sink into the ground, making the project even more costly. So, Russia may be leading discoveries so far this year, but extraction is another issue entirely.

Christina paused, then she said, "Here's the second page;

it talks about Celarus...

"US companies just put Celarus on the oil and gas map for the first time. It is a huge discovery. In fact, it is a string of 14 discoveries so far. Celarus had already hit 6 billion barrels of oil equivalent in the Stabroek Block. The potential for Celarus is huge, with some estimating Celarus's future production at 750,000 within the next five years - which would put it on to a similar footing to Guyana."

Christina added, "So this nets down to Russia discovering oil, but it is hard work to extract it and Celarus discovering plenty through US companies."

"I'm not sure why that would be on the phone though?" asked Bigsy.

"It's an article from a newspaper, photographed. Just a lazy way to get the clipping, " said Christina.

"What it points to, is that there's some interest in all of this, probably from Russia."

"Yes, and it points to our friend in the Indian restaurant being Russian, too, " said Clare.

Freemasons

A man in the corner approached me for a match
I knew right away he was not ordinary
He said, are you lookin' for somethin' easy to catch
Said, I got no money, he said, that ain't necessary

Jacques Levy / Bob Dylan

Meet the Freemasons

"So, do any of us know any Freemasons?' asked Bigsy, " I only know Fred and Barney."

Christina and Clare looked at one another.

Christina chipped in, " I think I might know someone, but it would get complicated for me."

"Well, who then?" asked Clare, looking intrigued.

"An old flame, " said Christina, " from the Arkhangelsk days. We were together for a while."

"Complicated?" asked Clare,

" Well he split from me, so it shouldn't be, " said Christina, " And it was all school-style crushes back in those days. The thing is, his father was the Senior Warden in one of the Masonic Lodges in Arkhangelsk. It was called the Lodge of Jekaterina. Antanov was keen on the Masons too, although then was still very young to be involved."

"How will you contact Antanov?" asked Bigsy, " I mean, he could be anywhere, "

"I think I can contact him via the FSB, " said Christina, " Although it could wake them up to me again. They will probably want something in return."

"Can you just dial up the Russians, then?" asked Bigsy.

"You bet, they still pay me so you can imagine they will want to keep an eye on me. To be truthful, it's the Americans that I've been careful to hide from, so your buddy Chuck Manners is a problem for me."

"Chuck? He's been in a similar position himself, needing to go to ground. Unless you've done something directly to him, I would think you'd be all right, " said Bigsy.

Handler

Christina thought long about her next move. She could ask Fyodor Kuznetsov, her handler, to contact her. It would restart her direct dialogue with the FSB, which was something she had tried not to instigate.

Kuznetsov's code name was Blackbird, which Christina didn't think was all that smart. Blackbird was just a little too close to 'blacksmith', which was the English translation of Kuznetsov.

Still, he had left her alone, and the money continued to roll in, so being asked for something in return for access to her Masonic friend was the right trade.

Christina rang the number for Kuznetsov. A London-based car dealership answered. "I'm interested in taking on of your vehicles for a test-drive, " she continued, " A hatch back."

There was a pause on the line and then a recorded voice asked for her reference code and the nature of her enquiry.

She gave a number, and after a moment was connected to a voice.

"And how may I help you today?'

"I'm seeking a colleague, " she began.

There followed a protocol to verify security, and then Christina waited.

"Eventually a voice said, " Hello, Christina? - Or should I call you Archangel?"

"Fyodor, " she replied, " It's been a while."

"Four years, actually, you have done a wonderful job of becoming invisible."

"Is everything okay?" he asked, " It is so unusual for you to make the initial contact."

"Everything is fine. I'm back in London now."

"What, no more Amsterdam?" he sounded surprised.

"Not now, and I've been keeping a low profile. I wanted to contact one of my friends from the Academy," continued Christina, " Antanov Chekeryn."

"Ah yes, he was in your group. From St Petersburg, I recall, his father was also a high-ranking member of the FSB. Well-connected around St Petersburg."

"What is the reason for your link?" asked Fyodor.

"I heard he was looking for me, " Christina lied, " We used to be more than just friends back in the Academy."

"Yes, he has moved back to Europe, " said Fyodor, " He was in South America for several years. I will attempt to contact him. If I am successful, how shall I arrange that you speak to one another?"

"Phone is fine, " said Christina, " Two Russians chatting by phone, nothing unusual."

"Okay, we have a number for you here."

"I'll give you my latest one, I'm not sure your system will have been able to keep up."

She recited the number to Fyodor, who recited it back.

"Okay, leave it with me, " he said, " You'll know in a week- *uspokoysya, beregi sebya, detka*"

"You stay safe too, " answered Christina.

Connections

Christina sat with Antanov Chekeryn.

They both ordered vodkas.

"za zda-ró-vye, " they said as they chinked glasses, " to your health."

"Za nashe khorosheye zdorov'ye i zdorov'ye nashikh kolleg v Arkhangel'ske, " said Antonov, *"For our good health and the health of our colleagues in Arkhangelsk,"*

"You are looking great, " he said. This western lifestyle suits you. Do you live in London now?"

"Yes, thank you, you look good yourself. I've moved around on various assignments for the FSB, life is never dull after you've been to Arkhangelsk, is it!?"

"No, I've also travelled widely. They sent me to South America. I was in Chile, then Ecuador, and then Brazil. I think they called me a disruptor. Brazil was far more expensive than the other two countries and Ecuador was the least expensive. It was strange in Brazil. There was a lot of German spoken. I think some transfers there were from Europeans after World War II. Nowadays I'm in Brussels, I've got a job in the EU. Then Blackbird called me and said I needed to come to London to meet Archangel. Said it was important."

"Yes, well thank you for coming over, and at such brief notice; I think this situation might intrigue you, " she grinned towards Antanov.

"Let me ask you, did you keep any links running with the Masons during your time in South America?" asked Christina, " I remember your father was into it."

"Yes, I did, actually, Chile, Ecuador and Brazil all had a Masonic presence - as the son of a Russian Senior Warden, they treated me like a special guest. I was initially quite surprised, but it looks as if the French were involved in the establishment of the Order over there.

"To be honest, it made my life so much simpler, being able to go to the meetings and find out what was happening from the well-connected people who attended. It's what my father did in *Sankt-Peterburg* to find out what was happening. Coincidentally, I've just joined the Grand Orient de Belgique. It's odd for such a small country that they seem to have about four different types of Freemasonry - it is like the EU all over again.

"And one for the women, no doubt?" asked Christina.

"Yes, they've a Women's Grand Lodge too, " nodded Antanov.

Antanov moved closer to Christina. He looked into her eyes.

She smiled back, " It's so good to be with a Russian man again, " she said.

"I was thinking just the same about being with a sexy Icelander, " he whispered, " Maybe we still have unfinished business?"

"Business. That's not the word I would use" said Christina.

She leaned towards him, and they kissed. Ever so briefly, but enough to set a tone.

"Power plays; they say the Masons isn't clandestine, but it is, and factional too, you'll see obedience cropping up in the descriptions of the Women's Lodges, " continued Antanov.

"You remember in Arkhangelsk there were two different Masonic houses? It was the same in Brazil. There was the Grand Orient of Lavrado Valley and the Grand Orient of Benedictino Valley, the former inclined to Roman Catholicism, the latter opposed to it.

"By 1872 the two parties had united but the following year they divided again. Catholics and Lutherans, one could say.

"After various arguments, by 1914 the Grand Orient exercised authority over 390 constituent Lodges, while England, Germany, and Italy were also represented.

"Wow, " so it wasn't difficult to stay connected, then?" asked Christina.

"Not really, although some of our Russian Order was subservient to the Germans and used the Adonhiramite Rite in our meetings. It was strange, we'd have their degrees and yet use French names."

"I can tell you are still fully up with all of this, " said Christina.

"Yes, I'm no Past Master, in fact I'm rather Select, " he said, " …that was a Masonic joke."

Christina shrugged, " Boys and their toys, if you ask me."

"I'd forgotten your forthrightness!" he smiled, " So what is it you want me to do with the British Freemasons, then?"

"Infiltrate, please, we need to find out what is happening. Something is wrong."

"I guess I'll need more than that. Does it mean I must spend some time here in London?" asked Antanov.

"Yes please, " said Christina, " I might even have some room for you at mine."

"Well, there's an offer I can't refuse, " replied Antanov.

He picked up his glass, " *Vot chtoby proytis' po goryashchim mostam!*"

"Yes, " said Christina, " Here's to walking over burning bridges."

Eight Mechanisms

The next morning, Clare visited Christina's apartment.

"Hey Christina, we thought you'd better come around to our office and brief everyone together. With your friend Antanov."

Christina invited Clare into the flat. Seated at the breakfast bar was Antanov. Clare admired Christina's choice. He looked suitably toned in his grey tee-shirt, with a pair of trainer bottoms, which could well have been Christina's.

"Hello, he said, " I'm very pleased to meet you. Christina has told me some things about you."

Clare listened to his accent; it sounded mid-European rather than Russian. Slightly upper-class. It fitted very well with London.

"I'm delighted to meet you too. Any friend of Christina's is a friend of mine. And she'd probably told you I go weak at the knees when I meet her friends' friends."

"Easy, tiger, " said Christina. Clare noticed immediately that Christina seemed particularly cheerful this morning.

Christina passed a black coffee across the kitchen surface to Clare.

Clare noticed that Christina was behaving just slightly more Russian this morning. Subtle, but noticeable.

"Okay thank you, Christina. When you are both ready, I'd like you to come over to our office in Hoxton. We call it The Triangle Works, but it's really a tiny old foundry which we adapted to make a pretty good base for what we do."

"It sounds great, " said Antanov, " I can be ready in about 15 minutes." He jumped up and left the kitchen.

Clare looked at Christina. Christina grinned back. There was nothing else to confirm.

"So where did you meet him?" asked Clare.

"Back in the day, " smiled Christina, " ...We were an item. Still best friends."

"I somehow worked that out, " smiled Clare.

Antanov reappeared, " Okay, ready, " he said. He was wearing a black leather jacket, still the grey tee-shirt but now had a pair of dark jeans. They walked to the elevator and down to the street where they could catch a cab to the office.

"Can I just check? Chuck Manners won't be at the office?" asked Christina.

"No, he is in London at the moment, met Jake yesterday, and they'll be keeping in contact, but there's no reason for him to be at our offices today."

They arrived, and Clare showed them into a meeting room. Jake appeared and was delighted to see Christina and greeted Antanov.

They shook hands and Jake said, " So you'll be telling us about Russian conflict strategies? - This could all be so useful to our understanding of what is happening."

Antonov was at one end of the table. "Sure, I'll take you though some of the basics. This is stuff that we present in FSB, but I'm sure the US presents almost identical thinking to the CIA."

"Christina's told me about this in the context of Raven - which as we all know has its fingers into everything related to energy, but oil in particular. That's what we'd call the big lever.

"It's a big lever because in Russia we take a view that oil fuels international conflict through eight distinct mechanisms. We know that is how the US sees it too, and that they are active to agitate these situations. Let's list them:

"1. Resource wars, in which states try to acquire oil reserves by force;

"2. Petro-aggression, whereby oil insulates aggressive leaders such as Saddam Hussein or Ayatollah Ruhollah Khomeini from domestic opposition, and therefore makes them more willing to engage in risky foreign policy adventurism;"

"I think you are saying that some messaging is manipulating the genuine reason?" asked Clare.

"That's right, " answered Antanov, " Let's see now, "

"3 Externalization of civil wars in oil-producing states ("petrostates");

"4 Financing for insurgencies—for instance, Iran funnelling oil money to Hezbollah;

"5 Conflicts triggered by the prospect of oil-market domination, such as the United States' war with Iraq over Kuwait in 1991;

"And then the making up of branded campaigns?" asked Jake.

"Precisely, and there has been no shortage of these from the Americans, " said Antanov.

"6 Clashes over control of oil transit routes, such as shipping lanes and pipelines;

"7 Oil-related grievances, whereby the presence of foreign workers in petrostates helps extremist groups such as al-Qaida recruit locals; and

"8 Oil-related obstacles to multilateral cooperation, such as when an importer's attempt to curry favour with a petrostate prevents multilateral cooperation on security issues. These mechanisms can contribute to conflict individually or in combination.

"That's why we always see conflict zones on TV shown with burning oil wells?" said Bigsy.

Antanov nodded, " I feel like I'm talking from an FSB manual when I say this, but these linkages between oil and international conflict are growing increasingly important in light of three transitions under way in global energy markets. The Americans are also troubled by each of these factors.

"The first is the shift in patterns of global oil production away from traditional suppliers in the Middle East and toward both suppliers of unconventional oil reserves in North America (like shale) and new suppliers of conventional oil, especially in Africa. As many as sixteen developing countries will become oil exporters in the near future, creating a swathe of new international security concerns. America and Russia are both concerned about this.

"Second, the low oil prices of the 1990s have given way to higher and more volatile prices, increasing the magnitude of the consequences one can expect from oil-conflict linkages.

"Third, the relative decline of U.S. hegemony may reduce the provision of public goods such as security of shipping lanes and pipelines. Although these transitions alter some of the ways in which the oil industry contributes to international conflict, none eliminates linkages between the two or allows the United States to disengage from global markets.

"Doesn't this all make for new sources of conflict?" asked Jake.

"That's right and some of them are unexpected sources of conflict, " Antanov nodded towards Jake and then continued, " It is important that policymakers think systematically about oil-security linkages when monitoring emerging security threats as the global oil industry transforms itself.

"As more countries export oil in the near future, new international dynamics will materialize, especially in Africa.

"Furthermore, if oil prices stay high, incentives for resource grabs will grow. Resource wars are most likely to occur in unpopulated territories or naval zones, as oil can be extracted from these areas without the need to manage a populated, potentially hostile territory.

"But what about the various blips over oil prices in the last few years?" asked Clare, " Like knock-on effects from the COVID-19 global pandemic?"

Antanov continued, " Yes, there are some wild fluctuations, but still an underlying sense of sensible pricing. There's almost too many variables, for some trading algorithms, but underneath it all there's a common-sense price point, which still allows the extraction and production to make a sensible profit."

"Thus, policymakers should be most concerned about disputed territories in the East China and South China Seas and naval borders in the Caspian Sea. There are already competing sovereignty claims to territory in those regions, and considerable uncertainty about the size of the energy resources located there, creating conditions ripe for miscalculation and mutual suspicion. There is already talk of testing weather-manipulating hardware from this region.

"What?" asked Bigsy, " How can anyone do that?"

"Both China and Russia have been experimenting with this technology and long had ways to make it work, " said Antanov, " For example, the Chinese have long had cloud chamber machines. In order for water vapour in the air to form clouds and eventually rain, it requires a nucleating particle.

"Typically, this is a tiny particle of dust which en masse produces the clouds we see in the sky. By artificially "seeding" the Tibetan Plateau with silver iodide particles the Chinese government is inducing the formation of clouds where there weren't any before. Once the clouds become unstable, this leads to artificially induced rainfall.

Each rain machine (chamber) is expected to create a 3-mile long strip of billowing clouds. When multiplied by the thousands of chambers China is installing along the Tibetan Plateau, it is estimated that China will be artificially controlling the weather over an area similar to the size of Alaska."

"But bring us back to the oil, " asked Jake.

"Well, I am in a way. Imagine weather manipulation of the sea-based oilfields. Policymakers should be especially concerned about security threats that arise from unexpected sources, such as allies' energy needs or benign actions that prompt hostile responses from rivals.

"It is only by appreciating these ways in which oil contributes to war can help policymakers design grand strategy, allocate military resources, and shape domestic energy policy.

"Many policy analysts focus narrowly on "energy security" as defined only by reliable access to fuel supplies, while missing the broader relationships between energy and security. Only by thinking systematically about the oil-conflict relationship can they craft intelligent foreign policy."

Box of Daylight

Step into the daylight and let it go

-Taylor Swift

Look around Raven

"Look. I've laid it out, but I can't see how these linkages tie together. Raven could be doing something, and clearly has an interest in energy, but why would it split itself into smaller organisations? It's not exactly a Bell Telecommunications monopoly situation." said Antanov.

"No, but there is something not right about this whole thing, " said Christina. The others nodded.

"So, you want me to dig around in Raven, but to look at their influence strategies?"

Antanov looked around the table, " And this is all because of a chance meeting between a Raven employee and a friend of Christina? It looks like a slender linkage."

"Well, there's clearly some other interest from Russia. We were followed when we discussed this with Nelson, " said Bigsy.

"The man carried a burner phone which only had a couple of entries. One about emerging oil-fields and the other was a Russian cell-phone."

"We didn't ring the number for fear of being traced."

"Well, I know a quick way of finding the number's origin, " said Jake.

"Unfortunately, it involves someone that I hear Christina isn't so keen to meet?"

"What, Chuck?" Asked Clare.

"Seriously?" said Bigsy, " I don't think Chuck would be put out to meet Christina. In fact, I think he'd be rather intrigued."

"It's not so much Chuck as the set of people behind him, " said Christina, " I think they would like to meet me and find out about a few things from my past."

"I think the same could be said of Chuck, " answered Clare, " I think we have a standoff!"

"What, like in Red Dead Redemption on PS4?" asked Bigsy, " That Mexican gambling scene, where a character says, 'There must be a name for this…' to which the Lee Van Cleef type called Landon Ricketts replies 'An impasse, sir. An impasse.' "

They all looked around the table. None of them knew what Bigsy was talking about.

"How about if I test Chuck on it?" asked Jake, looking for a way forward, " If Chuck says it's cool, then I'll believe him. After all, we've helped him out enough times."

"He told me yesterday that he was keeping Washington DC hours whilst he was over here, so I guess it'll be another couple of hours before I can call him at his hotel."

Chuck awoke to the sound of his phone. It wasn't the alarm. Someone from London was calling him.

"Jake?" he queried as he picked up the phone.

"Hi Chuck, thanks for yesterday and all. There's been some developments. Someone has re-appeared. Someone you might feel a need to turn in. She's a trusted ally of us though and we wanted to see whether we could persuade you to work with her in our team?"

"Her?" said Chuck, shaking his head from side to side, " You know I'm on Washington time?"

"Yes, I factored that in."

"Maybe not the late breakfast, though, " answered Chuck.

"Her, She, its Voronin, isn't it, " said Chuck, " I remember you worked with her when she was that singer, what was her name - Christina, er Christina Nott?"

"Katarina Voronin is how I remember her and that she was one slick operator, " said Chuck.

"I don't know the name Voronin, she's always been Christina to us, " answered Jake.

"Yes, well we found out that Voronin was a clever alias used by her along with at least two other women. They all looked similar, and it meant they could be in different places at the same time, which was helpful for alibis. A coupled of the Voronins were terrorists and assassins. I think the third one was more linked with security and covert operations. Finding out the head honcho in crime syndicates, that type of thing."

"Anyway, I'm sure that the CIA pulled the Voronins at least a couple of years ago. I think it will be case closed now, so nothing to see - let alone report."

"So, are you saying that you'd work alongside Christina without feeling the need to shop her to the US Agencies?" asked Jake.

"I don't think I could be much plainer. I know her as Voronin. The two Voronins have been apprehended. The case is closed, " answered Chuck.

"Anyway, I'd love to meet this person, she is a legend."

Politics in big fat cars

Bernard Driscoll was in his car being chauffeured to the next meeting. It was hard not to feel important when the powerful Jaguar was escorted by a couple of dark Range Rovers and two motorcycle outriders.

Despite a few unfortunate gaffes in his past, his luck was on the ascendency now. He was in some of the most influential Cabinet meetings and rubbed shoulders with the Prime Minister. If they wanted someone to set the scene on an important agenda topic, then he would be called to handle the early slots on BBC Radio Four. Why he had even been invited to take part in that hard-talking interview series on BBC World Service.

Driscoll thought back. It was since that chance meeting at the defence show. He had met a woman there who had introduced him to a supplier to Royal Kingdoms. That supplier had introduced him to a special men's meeting in East London and they had invited him to join their regular meetings.

He'd been wary of going to the men's meeting to begin with, but the supplier had urged him that 'it's not like that, " so he'd taken the plunge. It was in a pub in

London, reputedly close to the site of the Devil Tavern, which had been the place where Masons met in the 1700s.

Driscoll had been surprised to enter the pub and to see many men of around his age who were drinking and animatedly talking together. He thought he recognised a few from around Parliament, plus a couple of police chiefs talking loudly together.

"The great and the good, " he thought as he turned towards the person standing beside him at the bar.

"First time?" asked the person, " It's all a bit much isn't it? I'm William Whitehead, by the way, I practice law across the street there." He gestured out of the window of the pub and Driscoll could see the Royal Courts of Justice just across the street from the pub.

"And you are?" he asked.

"Ah yes, Driscoll, Bernard Driscoll, MP actually."

"There's quite a few of you here, this evening, I wonder if you go around in packs?" quipped William, " Look - let me introduce you to some others - don't worry, I'll steer away from the Parliamentarians."

He showed Driscoll into a small group of suited men, " Hello chaps, here's a fresh one, Bernard Driscoll from the Cabinet Office."

Driscoll monetarily wondered how William had worked out he was a Cabinet Minister, but then assumed his fame preceded him.

The group shuffled around to make an additional space for Charles to join in, and he soon found himself engrossed in a conversation about helping countries after warfare.

He left those distant thoughts and wondered instead at how time had moved on, as he watched the evening London traffic as he rounded Parliament Square. He would be driven inside the Parliament complex and then could make his own way through the tunnel back to his office in the newer construction of Portcullis House.

Yes, he had been quite a hero when he'd managed to get that arms deal concluded which involved many new British jobs to complete the munitions to be shipped to a middle eastern country.

Then he'd been able to facilitate the reparations project for the land area partially destroyed in an American bombing, also in the middle east.

And his track record was further enhanced as he persuaded the development of a new oil pipeline across the desert in Algeria and onwards towards Morocco.

The British engineering support that could be provided to the Iberian Peninsula was second to none.

Of course, he knew he'd need help to pull off these feats, but that's where his new friends and contacts were proving invaluable. He now knew just about everybody, it seemed. Why even his move to Portcullis House from Parliament was a stroke of good fortune from the Masons. He's only been talking in there one day about the school dinner smell that he had in his office and then, the very same week he was told that he was moving across the way.

Something that he'd noticed but was a pure coincidence,

was that several of the big contracts for oil pipelines, the munitions and that city reparations had all gone to subsidiaries of Raven.

But he had no interest in the firm, didn't own shares in them and wasn't on their boards. No need to declare anything at all in the members interests' pages.

He just arrived at Parliament's drop-off point. A police officer opened the door for him. "Good evening, Mr Driscoll, "

…Yes, this was the life.

Amanda Miller

Amanda's phone rang. She was sitting in her office in SI6, south of the River in Vauxhall Place.

"Amanda?" came a voice, " It's Chuck, Chuck Manners."

"Chuck Manners? I thought you were dead. After that bomb in London - outside of Bank of England? I should have guessed?"

"Yes, I'm back working with Jake, Clare and Bigsy, " he said, " I hope that's enough information to verify that it is really me?"

"Okay, I was just getting ready to ask you some security questions. You are still the same!" she smiled to herself. Chuck seemed to be in a hurry - as usual.

"What's the situation then?" she asked.

"A UK company running interference into the middle east."

"Oh yes, and who would that be?"

"I can't quite say at the moment."

"How widespread?"

"Oh, this is pretty wide and involves some leading politicians."

"Well, I take it you don't want to storm anywhere on UK soil at the moment, so what do you want?"

"I just want a phone number traced, " answered Chuck, sheepishly, " I know what you are thinking. It's not one of my more outlandish requests."

"Sure, " said Amanda, " And in return?"

"D'you know what?" said Chuck, " I'd like to take you to dinner."

Amanda was not expecting this. Chuck had usually seemed so preoccupied with his missions.

"I accept, you give me the number and I'll bring along the contacts details."

"How about Sheekey's?" asked Chuck.

"I'm impressed, you know your London restaurants, "

"They do a fine oyster too, " said Chuck.

J Sheekey

They met just outside the restaurant at precisely seven pm. Chuck greeted Amanda, they kissed on both cheeks.

"That kissing thing is so European, but it's catching on in parts of America now, too, " said Chuck.

"We might as well make the evening have a little frisson, " said Amanda, " It's been an age since I last saw you. I assume you have traversed the globe a couple of times in the interim?"

"Less than you might think, " said Chuck, " Remember I had to do a disappearing act after that London bomb."

They were shown to their table. "An outside one, if you'd prefer?"

They looked at one another, " Yes that would be great, " answered Amanda, " Look there's heaters too."

"Even blankets - this is better than the Marines, " smiled Chuck.

"They say that Ian Fleming wrote the James Bond books not while sipping martinis, but over oysters and a black velvet – that's Guinness and Champagne - or two in Covent Garden, at J. Sheekey." Said Amanda, " True or not, this ought to be the place for it."

Chuck looked around. Inside he could make out the leather banquettes and wood-panelled walls covered in framed photos., quite a few of which featured well-known faces.

"Well, I don't know about you, but I'm in the mood for seafood, " said Chuck.

"Well, I'm in the mood too, " flirted Amanda.

They ordered a dozen oysters and then fish for two. A sommelier appeared and Chuck discussed wines with him before ordering a Meursault - Les Tillets - Pierre Labet.

"I know it is a bit fancy, but you Brits, you seem to have no end to the lengths of your wine lists, " said Chuck.

"I feel very flattered by all of this, " said Amanda, " I guess this number and name must be very important to you."

"Not quite as important as this chance to be with you, " said Chuck, slightly clumsily.

Amanda laughed and so did Chuck who said, " Well, that is, if I had a better scriptwriter"

They enjoyed the meal and the ambience and made light chatter. They both kept a studied professionalism about what they could discuss but felt easy in one another's company. Chuck reached his hand across to touch Amanda's.

"This is a wonderful evening, " he said, " And you know how to relax me."

Amanda smiled; she was deciding but had almost made up her mind. The bill arrived.

Chuck took Amanda's hand and they left the restaurant.

"Can we make this last a little longer?" he asked.

"I'd love to, " said Amanda.

Chuck hailed a cab and they climbed in.

Mondrian

Amanda awoke, she had to remind herself where she was. It was a room overlooking the Thames in a modern hotel called The Mondrian. It had been the offices of a sea container shipping firm and had received one of the most stylish makeovers in London. It was just along the river from The London Eye.

She looked around. Chuck was outside, sitting in a chair on the balcony.

"I didn't want to wake you, " he said, " My plans to stay on Washington time went haywire yesterday."

"I think I might know something about that, " smiled Amanda, " So, Chuck, you seem to be away from the life here? Is that so?"

"Not really, " he replied, " I think I've reached - what's that hackneyed phase - 'Mastery' so I can do my role but still relax for the rest of the time."

"Well, thank you for a wonderful evening yesterday, "

"And thank you for being a lovely guide to this busy city,"

They kissed lightly.

"I suppose I should look at that contact that you gave me yesterday, " said Chuck, he flipped open the small piece of paper.

<<Oskar Hermann, Stuttgarter Straße 8A, Böblingen D-71032 Germany>>

"German, " he said, " Interesting."

Stuttgart

"Let everything happen to you
Beauty and terror
Just keep going
No feeling is final."

Rainer Maria Rilke

Triangle Works

Jake's phone rang. It was Chuck.

"Any luck?" asked Jake

"Oh yes, in more ways than one, " answered Chuck.

Jake mentally edited his next reply, " Excellent, so who is the lucky recipient of our tail's phone calls? And hold on I'm putting you onto speaker so that Bigsy and Clare can hear too."

"It makes little sense, " said Chuck, " It is someone in Germany, in a place called Böblingen."

"Böblingen?" said Bigsy, " I know Böblingen. It's next to where we had to pick up that car. You remember, Clare, when we picked up the new car from the Mercedes factory?"

"I remember, it's close to Stuttgart...Sindelfingen, that's where the factory was, but we stayed overnight at that hotel in Böblingen."

"Oh yes, I'd forgotten that you two went to pick up the blue car, factory fresh, " said Jake.

"It was a very interesting trip. Fly out, go to the factory, get a factory tour, then get delivered a brand-new car by literally the men in white coats."

"Yes, and then we went to that restaurant…" said Clare.

"Oh yes, the asparagus one. Spargel, " remembered Bigsy, " Spargel with everything. Spargel Suppe, Spargel Salat, Spargel as vegetable and then Spargel for pudding. That was an unusual experience."

"Remember that British guy at the next table? He was being entertained there by a computer company. I thought he would explode at the thought of asparagus with everything. Like a revenge of the Spam song."

"Oh yes, I think they placated him with steak and a lot of red wine in the end. Although they were very proud of their white asparagus and said they celebrated it through the whole of May, " said Clare.

"We made up for it by diverting through Champagne country on the way back. No luggage so we had plenty of boot space."

"Much as I enjoy hearing your reminiscences, we need to know what to do now that we've found the only person who the tail seemed to know., " said Jake.

"I think we need to contact this person, " said Clare, " Maybe we should do another Bigsy and Clare expedition, like the time we found Darren Collins in Zurich?"

Bigsy nodded, " Yes I'm fine about going out to Stuttgart, we can hop a flight from Heathrow."

"You know what, " said Clare, " I think this time it might be better if I go with Christina."

"How so?" asked Jake.

"Well, think about it. The guy following us was probably Russian. We could find out that Oskar has Russian connections too, it would be better for Christina to be able to follow what was happening."

Chuck's voice crackled on the Polycom, " Clare has a point - Christina also knows how to handle herself if things get difficult. Excellent, we have a plan."

The three in the office looked at one another. Clare would need to call Christina. Chuck seemed to be okay about her and Christina also seemed good with the idea of Chuck being involved. They would have two state operatives, one from Russia and the other from the USA, working together on a Triangle case.

"This can't get much more bizarre, " mused Jake.

"Trust me, it can!" replied Bigsy.

Clare called Christina. "Hey Christina - It looks as if we are on. We'll be visiting this strange contact in Germany. We fly to Stuttgart and then cab it to Böblingen. The address is very central."

Christina replied, "That's fine. Although this is one of the slenderest leads I've ever followed. A single number in a burner and then an address supplied by SI6, via a friendly US contact. I should have alarm bells ringing everywhere. But you know what? Let's do it."

Böblingen

They arrived at a roundabout in central Böblingen. There was a bakery on one corner and a couple of hotels on the others. The junction seems to be at the top of a hill.

"Now we need to find 8A, " said Clare, " It looks as if it is this way."

They walked along the street. It was soon apparent that the numbers were erratic. 8A was an apartment building along a side street. They looked at the entrance hall. There was a large post box with maybe 40 compartments.

"Oh my god, " said Clare, " I wasn't expecting this."

Christina was less phased by the apartment's size, having spent many years living in much larger blocks around Arkhangelsk.

"We'll just look through the names on the entry phone, " she said, " What are we looking for? Ah yes, Oskar Hermann…" She looked across the various bell pushes and at the individual boxes where mail could be left.

"Well, look, " she eventually said, "Here he is, flat number 14, see there's some mail for him."

She picked up the mail and looked through it.

"Interesting, it doesn't look like an agent lives here. This is all too routine, a couple of bills, and a magazine about golf."

She showed the papers to Clare.

"Now the question is, do we ring his door? To see if he is inside?"

"I'd say yes, said Christina. It is the most straightforward way. We can tell him the story we've made up."

"Ok, then, we'll ring the bell"

"Ja? Wer ist da?" came the reply.

"Hi, we are here to meet Oskar."

"Moment mal, "

They could hear someone being called.

"Could you stand outside the door, so that I can see you, please?"

They walked outside of the entrance and stood looking up in the air, towards the balconies of the apartments.

"Okay, just one minute. I will come downstairs, " said the voice, " We can go across the road."

Christina and Clare looked at one another and then towards the elevator.

"There's a set of stairs to the left, " said Christina, " Just in case- you know."

They could hear the elevator start up. Go up to a floor. Doors opening, return to ground level.

The doors opened.

"Oh my god!" said Christina, " Pavel!"

"Hello, Agnessa Dobrayadoch!" he walked towards her and briefly hugged her.

"Hold on, I'm confused, " said Clare, " My name's Clare, who are you?"

"Hello, Clare, my name is Oskar Hermann, Agnessa and I go back a long way!"

"Let's walk around the corner to Café Frech. We can explain all."

Café Frech

They walked the fifty metres or so to the nearby coffee shop. Café Frech was bustling and clearly popular with the local clientele.

They each ordered a coffee. Clare looked around at the wide selection of cakes and other treats being delicately enjoyed by the patrons.

"I think this is one of the best coffee shops and bakeries in Germany, " said Oskar.

"Okay, explain, " said Clare, looking at both Christina and Oskar.

"I had no idea, " said Christina, " None whatsoever."

"Well, it is complicated, " said Oskar.

"Agnessa and I both attended the same Academy."

"Why are you calling her Agnessa?" asked Clare, " She's

Christina?"

"Yes, I am, " confirmed Christina, " But I was once Agnessa Dobrayadoch. For around eight years actually. I was in Russia at the time."

"But I thought you were from Holland?" asked Clare.

"No, I'm Icelandic, from near to Reykjavik."

Clare looked wild-eyed, " This doesn't make any sense."

"Well, you know that I had to change my name recently from Nott to Hyde? This was another example."

"We end up with quite a few aliases in our business, " said Oskar.

"Yes, it's the same with Pavel- He appears now to be called 'Oskar'."

"So, what were you doing in Russia?" asked Clare, " Some kind of spy thing? - It has to be that."

"Yes, you could say that. But Pavel and I were also 'loves young dream' together at that time."

"You know, that's why Blackbird called me to come along here, " said Oskar, " He said he'd checked the Arkhangelsk records and found that you and I were an 'item'."

"Well, we were pretty close, your father even helped my Mamma get that job at the Museum, " agreed Christina.

"Yes, and the very next week you broke up with me - I was devastated, " said Oskar.

"But not too devastated to become very friendly with Galinka a few weeks later. I can remember you two hanging around living on air and love, " smiled Christina. She leaned over and gently kissed Oskar.

The coffee arrived, " Drei portionen Kaffee, " said the server.

"Danke sehr, " said Oskar and smiled to her.

"Okay, so which names should we use?" said Clare, " Christina and Oskar or Agnessa and Pavel?"

"We should use our current names, " said Christina. Oskar nodded.

"I've only been Oskar for a few days, " he said, " You seemed to be able to disturb the ant's hill when you spoke to Blackbird!"

"How so?" asked Christina.

"Well, it looks as if that person whose phone you stole was another Russian agent. A tail. Mid-ranking - *sredniy* - I don't think he was that good, if you managed to steal both his wallet and his phone."

Christina sailed, " You forget how good I am!"

"I agree, and that was the other factor. Blackbird was worried that his tail of an important company insider was being disrupted by what turned out to be one of his own operatives. That's why he called me. I was in Frankfurt, embedded. I have a family now. I married Galinka, you know."

Christina smiled, " Congratulations, I'd not have known."

Clare said, " Yes, but why did the tail in London have your phone number in his burner phone?"

"That's just it, " said Oskar, " He didn't. I was told to become Oskar Hermann by Blackbird on Tuesday. To drop everything and to come along from Frankfurt to Stuttgart and then to stay in the Böblingen flat until Agnessa, sorry, Christina made contact."

"Blackbird's thinking was that Christina would be more receptive to what was happening if she could see someone she could trust."

"So, what is happening?" asked Clare.

"Look, I need to know how much to trust you, " said Oskar, looking towards Christina.

"Christina, will you vouch for Clare?"

"Of course, I trust Clare completely. We are also good friends."

"Okay, then I'll tell you more." He looked around the Cafe, as if taking stock.

"I think we can safely say we are not being followed here, " said Christina, " I looked on the way in for tails or plants."

"Okay, then I'll tell you what I know, " replied Oskar.

Oskar's tale.

Oskar began, " We have to remember the context. Celarus sits on the doorstep of Russia. It has been a dictatorship for years and the Americans have quietly shored it up, preferring a buffer zone between Europe and Russia.

"I can't quite visualise Celarus, " said Clare, " What area is it in?"

"Imagine the western borders of Russia, where it joins into Europe. It's along part of that, a corridor partly created by the *Reka Sozh* - River Sozh."

"Yes, the river name sounds like *сожжъ* - *sozhzh'* - which is a Russian word for 'the burned parts of a forest prepared for ploughing', " said Christina.

Oskar continued, " At first glance, the whole situation might seem surprising. Celarus is naturally presumed as a traditional ally of the Russian Federation, which also leads to its limited engagement with the European Union.

"Yet in reality, bilateral relations between Moscow and Celarus for many years now have resembled a game of tug-of-war, in which each side seeks to maximise their own benefits.

"For Russians, we would measure such benefits in political influence, while for Celarusians – in currency. As long as Moscow pays part of the sustenance costs of the Celarusian regime, the political flexibility for the latter remains limited, including the cooperation with EU states.

"I see; under Russia's influence, then?" asked Clare.

"Yes, and that applied to diversification of oil and gas supplies, " continued Oskar, " For years, the Celarusian economy was heavily subsidised by the Russian Federation and duty-free oil shipments were one of the fundamental instruments in that regard. This form of subsidy was gradually reduced because of the tax reforms in Russia, leading to the replacement of crude oil export duty fees with a mineral extraction tax.

"Cynics might say that no oligarch has managed to get over the top of Celarus, presumably because of Tomas Kutnavenko's ruling dictatorship. The Celarusian authorities put significant effort into silencing alternative sources of information not under their control.

"Most Celarusians do not have access to independent media and as a result, public opinion in the country is determined by the state-run media, which is mainly pro-Russian and anti-Western.

"Another example of social media influence, driven from Russia?" asked Clare.

"Yes, and with consequences. The most active opposition activists and journalists are often fined or sentenced to jail. Participation in an unauthorised demonstration may result in police detention or a fine, " continued Oskar, " That's when President Tomas Kutnavenko invited the foreign investors to have a poke around to find further oil."

"In return, the US Secretary of State, Mike Pompeo, provided a short-term deal underwriting the Celarus requirement for oil - like a bridging loan to cover any shortfall, " Oscar took another sip of coffee.

"This was a big win for the USA; they got to go prospecting and could also provide oil, in effect disadvantaging Russia. Celarus was also a way into the EU-pipelines for America, so altogether advantageous, if you didn't mind dealing with a dictator-state.

Christina chipped in, " I suppose for Kutnavenko, he got to have a few American planes in his country, as the merest hint not to be messed with."

Oskar said, " Yes, on one hand, Russia was determined to set up new supply framework and proceed with the signing of in-depth integration agreement with Celarus . On the other, Celarusians now had alternative supply source, which could outprice Russian crude."

Christina added, " That was almost CIA level disruption to the economics of the region."

Oskar continued, " Yes, but then, surprise. One of the American companies discovered a new oilfield. It's significant, a real game changer for Celarus. They can dispense with the US supply once they start bringing it on stream."

Oskar paused and looked at Christina and Clare.

Christina looked surprised. How could this Cadet have learned so much? Then she realised, he would probably think the same of her.

"So, what was the basis of the operation in London?" asked Christina, " They must have told you?"

Poor Nelson

Oskar looked around the busy cafe again.

"You've heard?" he said, " about Nelson Redmund?"

Christina and Clare shook their heads.

Oskar continued, " They found his body. By a canal in Central London. They said it looked like a random crime. A robbery that went wrong."

"Nothing random about it, " said Clare, " Nelson seemed pretty grounded and savvy."

Christina and Oskar looked at one another. Clare could see they were weighing up the method.

"Yes, too much co-incidence in all of this, " said Christina, " Nelson was also our original lead into this."

"What about his buddy, Javel?" said Clare, " Do you think he would know any more?"

"I think we'll need to find out what the Russians know, via Blackbird, " said Christina, " There must be an angle on this, after all, they were tailing Nelson and bothered to send Oskar to meet us."

Oskar nodded, " I agree, I'm getting a strong feeling that this is dangerous now."

Ask the Russians

*'Sometimes it is necessary to be lonely
in order to prove that you are right.'*

Vladimir Putin

A place by the lake

"Are you staying in town?" asked Oskar.

"Yes, we've a place down by the lake. It's a small hotel where we've a couple of rooms. I think we could walk there from here."

"Okay, give me until tomorrow. I'll see what I can find out, " said Oskar.

They parted from the cafe and Christina and Clare walked together down the hill, past several other shops.

"What did you make of that?" said Christina to Clare.

"Some things I didn't know, " giggled Clare, " About you and him. Christina with a boy in every town. Antanov, Oskar…"

"Stop it, " said Christina, " I can't help it if they all fall at my feet. You know something:

Время для бизнеса, час для веселья - *Vremya dlya biznesa, chas dlya vesel'ya.* - time is for business, the hour is for fun, as the Russian saying goes."

They had reached to end of the hill and were standing near a busy road junction. Ahead they could see the lake.

"Over there, to the right, that's where our hotel is., " said Clare.

"But what did you think about the whole situation?"

asked Christina again.

"Complicated and messy. I can see the Russians would want to get involved if they thought that Celarus would become a threat. Another American aircraft carrier."

"Except its land locked, " said Christina.

"Okay a military base then, " said Clare.

"Yes, America wins big time - they get to put in military, to exploit the resources via their own companies and to wrest some oil control from the Russians, " said Christina.

"Won't that divide your loyalties though?" asked Clare.

"Ask me again tomorrow after we hear what Oskar has to say."

…

The next morning, they were back in Café Frech.

"It's no good, I'm going to have some breakfast here, " said Clare.

"It's great, " said Oskar, " They do a breakfast basket, with the typical German breakfast items in it. I recommend it."

They ordered three Frühstuckkörble and then turned to Oskar.

"So, what did you find out?" asked Christina.

"Well, first Blackbird didn't seem to know so much, but I

think that was his training to not tell us anything. I decided it was best to say you were in danger, Christina, just to make him open his mouth more. I told him that after Nelson we suspected that you were next on the hit list."

"I also discovered that Nelson's death was not anything to do with us - Blackbird had been as surprised as us to find out when he was killed."

"That helped loosen Blackbird's tongue; he said he thought the plan was related to the divestment. It turns out that the person following you that evening was from Russian Intelligence. His name *Марк Лисон* - Mark Leeson, was as burnable as his phone. Blackbird said he was a temporary asset set to work as a tail."

Christina remembered her training from the Academy. The Russians had a long list of agent types, mainly because some of them were for a single purpose. She could remember being annoyed at how long it took to remember them all.

Clare said, " Leeson? Wasn't that the name of Rogue Trader? I see the FSB have a sense of humour."

"Yes, well I asked Blackbird directly what the agent's code name was. He took a while to answer, but finally came back with "Olivier."

Christina laughed, " Now that's what I call a quick snack!"

Clare looked confused, " What's so funny about his name?"

Oskar was laughing too, " Olivier - Russian Salad - Take

boiled potatoes, boiled eggs, ham, meat cut into cubes, green peas, mayo - This is not haute cuisine; rather, a quick snack when you don't want to treat your guests to a "real salad." That's why it's so popular during New Year celebrations. It's easy to cook, and not as tasty as you think."

"Do you think that were having a laugh when they handed out the code names?" asked Christina, " Say Oskar, what's your code name?"

Oskar smiled as he said, " Sable - very high class! And what about you, Christina, what's your codename?"

Christina smiles, " Archangel, " she said, " Arkhangelsk."

Oskar's expression changed, " No way, " he said, " I'm in the presence of the next Tsarina of the FSB, or at least a supergod legend. Everyone has heard of your exploits. Some even know your names - Katarina Voronin, for example."

"Don't believe everything you are told, " said Christina.

Clare looked at the two of them, engaged in spy-banter, " So do I get a name too?" she asked.

"Not unless you want to join the FSB, " said Christina, but let's think for a minute…*Clare, Клэр, бордо, кровь жизни, krov' zhizni, krov', boltun…" - How about "Magpie?"*

Oskar laughed, " I can see how you got to it. Clare, Claret, Lifeblood, *Krov' zhizni* - Crow, Magpie - all through the Russian. - But you know that Magpie is considered a chattery bird in Russian?"

Clare laughed, " Hmm I'm not sure how to take that, but

I'll go with Magpie for the moment, anyway."

They chinked their coffee cups together, " To Sables, Magpies and Archangels" said Oskar.

Okay, said Oskar, " back to the Russian salad. So, Olivier was tasked to follow Nelson. It was clearly something to do with Raven and the evolving situation in Celarus."

"That's why the Russians would be interested. They'd be rattled by the corporate moves of America."

"Well, we also know that Raven was getting ready for a divestment, to set up another company called Brant Holdings, " said Christina, " But I don't think Nelson knew much about this. He was asking us to do some digging."

"Yes, so the Russians followed Nelson around, mainly to see who he was speaking to, " said Clare.

"But then Nelson mysteriously dies, because of a suspected robbery. The coincidences are starting to stack up, " said Christina.

"I asked Blackbird if we could trace Olivier, " said Oskar, " He was hesitant, but gave me this address. Blackbird said he was worried that this whole thing was spiralling out of control."

He showed Clare and Christina a piece of paper. It was an address on Olympian Way, in the Greenwich Peninsula.

"Wow, " said Clare, " That's close to the Dome, let me check it on my phone, " She tapped away, " Yes, it's as I thought, the address seems to be an office block in the main O2 conurbation, facing across the river towards Victoria Docks."

"It looks as if they've given an accommodation address instead of where he lives, " said Oskar.

"It's still useful, " said Christina, " Who knows what we'll find there!"

"It should be our next port of call, " said Christina, looking to Clare, " Oskar, I guess you'll be staying here in Germany?"

"Well, technically, my assignment was over when I made contact, " said Oskar, " and Galina and the kids will be expecting me back in Frankfurt. It might take some explaining that I've been with two beautiful ladies, one of whom was an ex 'true love of mine.'"

Christina laughed, " Oh yes, when you were the great moody poet with a scarf. - A *lattelepjandi listamenn*!"

"You forget I don't speak Icelandic, " he said.

"Makes no odds, we are still first loves, " said Christina as she walked up to him and kissed him on both cheeks.

Clare then felt awkward, she was running out of farewell moves.

"Goodbye, Oskar, " And thank you, " she said.

He rose, hugged her and said, "Farewell, my little magpie."

Christina and Clare walked out of the cafe, aware that they were both drawing stares from the adjacent tables.

"Heathrow? I think Antanov might be feeling a little lonely" said Christina.

"Heathrow." Confirmed Clare.

Echterdingen

They sat in Echterdingen airport awaiting their plane. Christina was reading a magazine, and Clare was listening to music on her headphones. Someone approached.

"Christina?" he said, " Is it Christina Nott?"

Christina looked up. She recognised the face, but not from where.

"Amsterdam, " he said, " I'm Ian - I played guitar on some of your tracks. When we were making those copy tracks."

"Ian!" said Christina, " I remember, you had that hand-built raw-wood Telecaster. The one I borrowed. I even made a track with it - 'Telecaster blues (I only borrowed it)' "

"Yes, we were just doing a gig here in Tübingen - my band are over in the cafe - I spotted you and just wanted to say 'Hi' - you must get it all the time!"

"Not really, " said Christina, she waved across to the band, sitting in the cafe. They waved back and the female blew kisses to Christina.

"Can I? -Er - this sounds kind of lame - can I get a selfie with you?" asked Ian.

"Of course, you can - how about with Clare as well?" suggested Christina.

Ian set up his smartphone. They all crowded in. A flash and the picture was taken.

The airport announcement called for the flight to Heathrow.

"Great to see you; enjoy Amsterdam!" said Christina.

London, the Triangle offices.

Jake, Bigsy and Clare were sitting around a table.

Christina and Antanov walked in.

"Christina, I wasn't expecting you today, " said Jake, " And hello again Antanov, it's good to see you both, actually."

"Let's see if we can devise a plan, " said Bigsy.

Clare began, " Well, we know that Raven is splitting off Brant Holdings. That it has rattled the Russians. That a whistle-blower - Nelson - has been suspiciously killed. That the Russians tailed Nelson and have a base somewhere near to the Dome, on the Greenwich Peninsular."

"We also know that the tail for Nelson was a low-level Russian, not a killer, so I'm guessing that Nelson met his fate at someone else's hands, " added Christina.

Clare replied, "They must be hiding something. I'd have thought that Raven's sale of Qube to create Brant was a typical post-Brexit move? Shifting yet more British companies into Europe?"

Jake nodded his agreement, " 'Selling England by the Pound,' as a prog-rock group might say. It has been going on ever since Thatcher's Britain. One of the early ones was Vickers plc which sold Rolls-Royce Motors to Volkswagen Group, for £480m. I guess that opened the floodgates."

"That was under Tony Blair," added Bigsy, "Not Thatcher."

"Oh all right, Thatcher's privatisations – like of British Telecom opened the floodgates and then it took a while to catch on and for the lawyers to work out how to make it all seem legitimate selling a company so that the previous management could make a bundle," said Jake.

Bigsy could see that Jake was getting irritated, but Jake continued anyway, "Now it's difficult to tell who owns what in the high street, through a succession of packaging of sell-offs. It doesn't ma. There's Boots the Chemist sold to US company Walgreens as well as the well-known UK bookshop Waterstones now owned by Russians."

"The treasured NHS has American IT all over it and services from Southern Cross, which is in turn owned by Blackstone, the huge American Corporation."

"Step on a train and its likely to be run by Deutsche Bahn, SNCF, Keolis of France, Abellio from the Netherlands. Heck, even the Essex commuter train C2C is Italian."

Bigsy nodded agreement, "Apple UK is taxed through Ireland, MoD research spun off the high-tech Qinetiq which was then bought by Carlyle (with ex PM John Major on board) and the clever people at ARM semiconductor went to Softbank in Japan."

"I remember when Kraft bought Cadburys, and that the Royal Mail is German," interrupted Clare, "It says it on their vans."

"And most of our energy in the UK comes from German Eon, French EDF and Spanish Iberdrola," added Jake.

"Like BA," said Bigsy, "That's Spanish isn't it?"

"And it has been in all the papers about British Steel and that Chinese Company - Jinye, isn't it?" asked Clare.

"Ironic that," said Jake, "First they flood our steel markets, then they buy us up."

"Well Raven is lining up a similar move, hoping to go underneath Parliament's scrutiny, but maybe needs a tame minister to help it along."

"And that Raven is well connected, heck, its head office is kitted out like a Masonic Lodge, " added Jake.

"We've also got American involvement via Chuck and even SI6 interest, because he used one of his contacts there to get us the address in Germany, " added Clare.

"And Antanov, is well-connected in the Masons to help us find out more."

Antanov smiled, " We shall see how our 'interests'

converge or diverge? - Russia, The Masons, Raven. But good news, I've been busy while Christina was away. I've been invited to a Masonic meeting. They say it is officially a 'Ladies' Night', when the wives and partners of Masons can also attend."

"So, no real business will be transacted then?" asked Bigsy.

"Correct, but it is a great way to meet people and, in my case, to find out about joining. And to top it all, it is at the Raven offices. Their Head Office in London."

"And another advantage. I can take along a lady."

Everyone around the table looked towards Christina.

"Oh, I see, Okay, yes then, " she said.

Ladies' Night

Now, if I was an actor or a dancer that was glamorous
Then, you know, an amorous life would soon be mine
But now the tinsel light of star break
Is all that's left to applaud my heart break
And eleven o'clock I watch the network news

Goodnight ladies, ladies goodnight
It's time to say goodbye
Let me tell you, now, goodnight ladies, ladies goodnight
It's time to say goodbye

Lou Reed

Infiltrate

They were back at Christina's flat.

"Okay Antanov, so what do I need to know about this Ladies' Night at the Masons?" asked Christina.

"It'll be glitzy, and quite formally structured. Although a few lodges that accept women as members, the traditional lodges still maintain a men-only membership.

"It is more of an evening gowns and frock kind of night, the fancier, the better. It's the perfect time to bring out the jewellery as well. If you want to really impress, wear a small brooch with a rose on it. It is a signal of power.

"I hope you are thinking of 'Eyes wide shut' by now?"

Christina smiled, " Well, I wasn't and I'm assuming we don't get the kinky bits either?"

"No, it's pretty staid, except for the conversation. Evening gloves are about as kinky as it gets. They are part of the tradition. They should worn until grace is said, after which, they can be taken off.

"Once we arrive, we will be presented to the Worshipful

Master and his Lady. Make sure you have something nice to say to the Lady, to create a good impression. Because I'm a son of a high-ranking Mason, it should also mean we get to sit at a good table.

"And I can talk to anyone about anything?" asked Christina,

Antanov replied, " Yes, use your instincts for that part, it doesn't matter if you ask a few probing questions about Masonic things, either. Most women are fascinated to know what their men-folk are up to with their strange leather aprons and their chisels."

"At the start of the meal, everyone is to stand behind their chair and wait for the Director of Ceremonies to bang the gavel or ring a bell. After the signal, the Chaplain will say grace. Usually there's a few ushers to remind you of these things.

"My quick description is to think of a traditional wedding reception with service à la russe."

"Got it, " said Christina.

"The Rose Song is a regular part of Ladies' Night. Here, roses are presented to the Master's Lady, after which toasts will be made. See why the rose brooch is important. And by wearing it you are showing a power and daring.

"I doubt whether a single other woman would do so. I'm going to find you a particularly powerful rose symbol, with a cross, triangle and an ankh. The Lady will notice it.

"After this, the men often have a song prepared for their ladies. There will also be presents, and speeches will be made. The rest of the night can be used for further fellowship.

"Okay, " said Christina, " So what kind of gown? I can go traditional style Diane von Fürstenberg or wild-child Wunderkind?" She flicked on to her smartphone.

"Here, I saved these pictures as examples?"

Antanov took a look, " Oh. My. God. He said at the first picture - That's Wunderkind. You will blow their minds if you show up like that. Too edgy by halves. I love it."

Then he looked at the Fürstenberg, " That's the right kind of slinkiness. You can still own the room in that one, without causing a riot."

Christina laughed, " I had a feeling you'd pick that one. The blue one says it should be worn with sandals though, but I was hoping for Louboutin."

Handshakes

They arrived back at the now-familiar entrance to the Raven Head Office. They had come by taxi and there were several other glamorous looking types also arriving. Outside, the security seemed to have been beefed up and men in dark suits with small radio packs were marshalling those entering. There was a funnel that led to a short red carpet. Everyone seemed to have brought their invitations along.

"Antanov? We do have some tickets somewhere?" asked Christina.

"It's fine, " he said, " I have the right handshake, " He winked towards Christina.

"Hello, you have your ticket?" asked one of the security people. Antanov took the security man slightly to one side and said something quietly to him.

"Oh, Sir, please come this way, we have a special entrance for special guests."

Antanov gestured to Christina who slipped out of the line. They followed the security man to a different door.

"Here, he said, " Special guests' entrance, "

They pushed at the door and instantly were inside a spacious lobby. There were golden columns and a photographer already snapping their pictures, "

"Hello, " greeted a woman in a dark gown, " Wow that blue gown is stunning, " she said to Christina, " Could I have a photo with you - you don't mind?" she shot a look to Antanov, who nodded approval.

"Here, now take some of this champagne. Look I'd like to present you both with these small brooches to wear; it helps identify you in the room - as special guests."

Christina looked at the brooch. It had a small picture of a spring of acacia on it.

"And this means?" she asked. She noticed that Antanov had a different symbol, his was a more traditional compass and set square, in gold but outlined in red.

"Yours is a symbol of Immortality of the soul and innocence, " he began, " Mine is more or less a symbol of rank and how long I've been a Mason. They are both pretty serious. You should wear the acacia brooch underneath the rose brooch that I gave you."

They paused to pin their brooches. They entered the main room from the side lobby and already there was an atmosphere of excitement. It seemed very different from the Head Office visit day with Nelson.

Christina could see that Antanov was instantly at ease with the proceedings, approaching various people to say hello and introducing Christina. He introduced her as his partner, which she did not mind, realising that the label was for simplicity of explanation. She remembered back to the Academy and thought about the briefings there on 'cocktail parties'. This was not anything like the session they described.

Eventually, it was time to sit down for dinner. Christina remembered about waiting until the Worshipful Master and his Lady had sat, the Director of Ceremonies had banged the gavel and a Chaplain had said grace.

She decided it was wise to say nothing of these events, even if she did think them arcane.

Then, as if on a signal, conversation broke out. Several men started to chat to her and Antanov appeared to be talking to a stunning blonde woman across the table from him. Christina looked either side of the blonde but couldn't decide who she had come along with. The scene had the appearance of a much younger woman with an ageing businessman, however she cut it.

One of the men proposed a small off the cuff toast to the lovely ladies present, and Christina thought she caught the blonde saying *"za zda-ró-vye"* - which intrigued her. Perhaps the woman was actually Russian - surely not the cliché of a Russian bride?

"…for a living then?" droned one of the men.

"Oh, I work in public relations, " said Christina, " It's for a very small firm, we help small businesses get started, " she replied, somewhat on autopilot, " oh and you?" she said feigning interest.

"I'm in one of those companies that specialise in mergers and acquisitions, actually, " he said, " We work mainly around the city, you may have heard of us? ISMC? International Strategic Management Consultants? We help bigger clients through the merger or divestment processes."

"Oh, that's very interesting, " said Christina, " I guess you get to see how many companies operate?"

"Yes, we are often in their board rooms, or their strategy meetings, all over Europe. My name is Gerhardt, by the way, Gerhardt Schmidt - from Germany."

"Oh, I was in Germany earlier in the week, near Stuttgart, actually, "

"I'm from Wiesbaden, which is close to Frankfurt. That's where we have our main office."

"In Germany? You have such an English or American-sounding name for the company?"

"Yes, branding, I think, to get the kind of coverage we want, es ist besser to have a London-sounding centre - still - even after Brexit!"

He laughed.

"So is your partner here?" asked Christina, looking around the table.

"Yes, she is, that is Nina, across the way, she is the one with the blonde Haar."

Christina thought for moment. Nina, a useful Russian name that does not sound out of place in most of Europe.

Another man had caught her eye, " I like your brooches, " he said, eyeing the acacia and the rose, for what Christina considered just slightly too long.

"Yes, I thought they were pretty to wear this evening, " said Christina, " and the acacia one was given to me on the way into the event."

"Ahah," said the man, " We are in the presence of honoured guests!"

"And yes, that's my partner, " Christina gestured to Antanov and saw the man take an eyeful of Antanov's regalia.

"Oh, I see, we have an honoured guest from another lodge here present this evening."

"Yes, Antanov is now in the Belgian Lodge, but before that was in the Brazilian Lodge. His father was an officer too."

The man seemed impressed by this, Christina thought to herself that the von Fürstenberg gown was working.

"So, I hear there is something happening with Raven? They get more successful but are planning to sell something?" ventured Christina.

"Really?" asked the man, " I wouldn't know about that. There's always rumours sweeping around."

"I know, I expect I've got it wrong, " said Christina, " This salmon is delicious - it tastes so fresh - it bursts in my mouth."

"Yes, it says in the menu that this is Icelandic salmon, something of a rare treat, " said Gerhardt.

Christina bit her tongue, she knew better than to answer

that particular point. She could see Antanov getting more deeply involved in his conversation with the blonde and another dark-haired woman who reminded Christina of Angelina Jolie, in a modest black dress, high to the neckline. Then she realised that 'Angelina' was the partner of a 55-year old balding businessman.

There was something unusual about these men's choice of partners. Christina decided that they were either all punching above their weight, or that the Ladies' Night was a thin excuse to bring someone else along.

She would have to wait until later to ask Antanov about this. She looked around the room, there was still a good smattering of 'reasonable match' husband and wife combos. Perhaps she had just landed on an usual table?

The evening continued. Several other men came along to chat with Christina, she could not work out whether they were simply being friendly, or whether there was something else at play.

She did not try any more direct questioning, although she found it useful to mention ISMC a couple of times, which got a reaction from whoever she was talking to.

Apparently, ISMC was known as a cost-cutter, as one man put it 'a butcher' who would strip out unwanted headcount. Christina could see how this would play to the Brant agenda. She was curious that here no-one was aware of any form of divestment, though. She wondered if it was a corporate secret, although in this area of free speech it seems that they would talk openly about other company secrets.

She found out that the Chairman had been replaced in an office coup. That the finance for the last five years was being inspected by HMRC. That someone had been sacked from energy trading for setting up a small cartel among the traders from other organisations and manipulating the forward price.

Christina decide that this was the stuff of big business, that nothing exceptionally bad seemed to be on the list, but there were undertones of corrupt practice.

She thought this was more likely to be a Raven thing rather than anything involving the Freemasons, who seemed harmless enough with their special leather aprons and impossibly long climb to the top of the organisation. 33 degrees to get to the top? It was worse than the Russian Army.

Then something happened.

A man who knew Gerhardt came to sit at their table. He was quite loud and seemed to know Gerhardt from a few trips abroad.

"Hello Bernard, " said Gerhardt warmly, " How was the Grand Prix?"

"Which one?" asked Bernard, " Hockenheimring or Monza?"

"Ah yes, " I'd forgotten you went to both circuits this year. I suppose we'll see you again at Abu Dhabi. - I hear the Yas Marina circuit has had no expense spared!"

Christina was intrigued by this. Bernard did not look like the kind of man who would be able to go swanning round the world to Formula 1 races. She always thought of the type of Russians that did this. Tanned, gold cufflinked shirts, gold bangles and women. This man was wearing a Seiko watch. Mail-order inexpensive practicality.

She also noticed the "we'll" in the phrasing. This was one of the old-corruptibles. An industrial tourist. Leveraged travel at a consultant's expense. In someone's pocket.

Now she had to guess what he did for a living.

She didn't have long to wait. Another man came along, " Bernard, how the devil are you? How's things in The House? Gerhardt, are you talking to Mr Driscoll about work things? - Naughty naughty. And let me introduce my friend Marion Charlotte."

Christina noticed a fairly ethereal looking woman walk over. She smiled at Bernard and said, " Yes Charles tells me you are an MP."

Christina could see that Driscoll was smitten by the soft charm of Marion and watched with fascination to see how it would play out. Driscoll's eyes were on stalks like a comedy cartoon character.

"I'm delighted to meet you, Ms Charlotte. This is a very special occasion isn't it? and Hello Charles, good to see you, " said Driscoll, " To answer your original question - Gerhardt is talking about Formula 1 racing. So, no harm done there.

"Sir Charles, a pleasant co-incidence to run into you here this evening!"

"If you could excuse me, gentlemen, I know something about Formula One racing drivers, but had better move before my ears start to burn!" Marion smiled to them all and lingered on the smile to the still popper-eyed

Driscoll.

Then she breezed on to meet another small group at the next table.

"Fascinating, " said Driscoll.

"Oh yes, she and one of the Formula One drivers were an item for a while. I think she could give you the insiders' track on the sport."

"Oh, it would be great to meet her for longer, " said Driscoll.

"Leave it with me old chap, " said Sir Charles, " You never know! Standing here it seems damn lucky that I was invited at the last minute, I think our firm are helping out to run the event and so they asked me if I could make an appearance"

Christina worked it out. Bernard Driscoll was some kind of minister in the House of Commons. And now these two fellows were working the old one-two with him. One to snare him and then to pass him along to a senior partner - "Sir Charles".

A senior partner who would add Marion Charlotte as a sweetener. And Driscoll didn't seem to have a clue that he was being played.

Christina remembered her Academy training - the western influence strategies. Cultural webs. Johnson and Scholes. Charles Handy. The so called 'cocktail parties'.

Oh yes, mark the senior players at an event such as this. Create a signalling system, for when there's an opportunity. Be prepared to stand down if the object realises what is happening. Inject the ideas at multiple levels, so that they will coalesce when the organisation gets back together.

Christina stood. Everyone looked towards her.

"Excuse me, gentlemen, " she said.

She was making her way to the washroom, but it was also partly to check on the organisation of this event.

She found the main signage. In very small letters underneath Ladies' Night, were the words 'sponsored by ISMC.' Okay, so they could probably have an input to the arrangements. Or maybe they had run the whole event to take the 'pain' away from Raven.

She was checking her makeup when the blonde woman appeared, " Hello, " she said, " We're on the same table, do you know Jennifer Sussex too?"

"Jennifer?" queried Christina, " Oh yes, Jennifer, I call her Jenny!" lied Christina.

"I thought so, " said the blonde, " My name is Natalie, " she held out a hand. They shook hands.

"It's good to get a few minutes break, but Jennifer will be around if we stay here too long, " she said, " that man I'm with is exhausting, he talks about golf all the time and wants to keep showing me hand grip positions."

"I've heard it called a lot of things, " said Christina, " but never that."

"Well, it's good money at these Raven events, so I can't complain, " said the blonde; she shook her hair, twisted on her heels and was gone.

Christina returned; Gerhardt was sitting alone. It was turning into one of those wedding dinners.

"Hello again, Gerhardt, " she said, " What happened to your two friends? - The one you called Sir Charles and the MP?"

"Oh, Sir Charles Frobisher and Bernard Driscoll; they walked over to one of the side rooms to discuss something. I have a horrible feeling it was work!" he laughed.

The old one-two thought Christina. One to catch them, the second to tie them up.

The Corruption of Bernard Driscoll

The next day, after the Ladies' Night, Christina and Antanov were trying to make sense of what they had discovered. They were around at the Triangle offices and sat together with Clare, Bigsy and Jake.

"What have we got?" asked Jake.

"Well, it's all rather strange, " answered Christina, " We need to work out how much of what we discovered was driven by Raven, how much by the Masons and how much via a firm, employed by Raven. They are called ISMC and are a German-based M&A consultancy."

"Mergers and acquisitions, what about divestments?" asked Clare.

"I think it amounts to the same thing, it's a case of buying and selling, " said Antanov, " From what we can make out, Raven have hired this consultancy. In turn, they are driving the agenda along, using various influence strategies. The Masons appears to be one of these approaches and they are using it to pick off some of the players needed to make whatever Raven is doing work."

"You are not defending the Freemasons in any way? We respect your loyalty to them but would prefer to know, " said Jake, knowing he was broaching a difficult subject.

"No, absolutely not, " said Antanov, " I'm as keen as all of you to find out what on earth is going on and to understand how the Freemasons are being misused, "

Antanov continued, " For example, let's say a company needs influence in government. Normally this would be through lobbying, but a more subtle attack could be by using some tamed and slightly corrupted MPs to drive the agenda along.

Christina picked up, " So now, we discover that Bernard Driscoll, who is the Member for Ilford Central and also a member of the Cabinet as Minister for External Relations and Chancellor of the Duchy of Windsor, is also a Formula 1 enthusiast.

"No big deal, except if he is able to go to a whole range of the races, in exotic locations, Germany, Italy and United Arab Emirates. These seem to be visits arranged by ISMC."

Antanov continued, " And we also noticed that there were some additional attractive partners at the Ladies' Night event. I'm not sure that Freemasons would countenance such behaviour, but one of the women mentioned to Christina that Raven paid well."

"Yes, and I did seem to be getting quite a lot of attention from roving single men, " said Christina.

"Antanov, tsk-tsk, " Clare waggled a finger toward him.

"I could see that Christina was ably looking after herself, and I was sitting next to her, " replied Antanov, " I had the impression that people thought our table had been stocked with some spare ladies."

Jake recapped, " So we seem to have some kind of corruption, operating at a top level, via the mechanism of a Masonic meeting, but one hosted by Raven and sponsored by ISMC."

"Did you get any additional contacts?" whilst you were at the event?" asked Bigsy, " People who we could trace or track down for their public history?"

"We did, " said Christina, " I talked to a contact at ISMC - a Gerhardt Schmidt, from their Frankfurt office. He also pulled over his boss, Sir Charles Frobisher. I get the impression that Sir Charles was a special deployment at this event. Schmidt seemed to be more like a low-level sales type, there to snare the big animals."

"So, we think that Driscoll is being manipulated?" asked Clare.

"Most certainly, " said Christina, " but we don't know by whom, nor why."

Masonic friends

"I'm going to make some calls, " said Antanov, " See if anyone knows anything."

"This is where the Rose comes in useful."

"I noticed that rose had a small golden cross in the background, " said Christina, " I thought I saw others were examining it. As a woman you get used to strange men staring at one's chest."

Clare nodded. Christina produced the small brooch from her purse along with the golden acacia twig.

"They are lovely, " said Clare,

"But no doubt there's some symbolism?" asked Bigsy.

"I like the touch of gold, " added Jake, pointing to the small golden cross subtly behind the rose. And a Triangle?

"Yes, " said Antanov. "I decided to give Christina a symbol, which would cause the others present to treat her well."

"The symbol is Rosicrucian, it's a Templar Cross, but in case this it doesn't look overtly religious. That triangle is another powerful symbol. The cross from which it is inspired pre-dates Christianity by about 1400 years.

"Hmm, the cross; I always wondered about the Christians using a Roman torture instrument as a sign of faith, in any case, " said Bigsy.

"Very cool, " said Clare, " but I've only heard of the Rosicrucians in that book by Umberto Eco - the one they made into a murder mystery. James Bond as the main investigator in a Benedictine monastery filled with too many monkish murder suspects. Agatha Christie in Church."

"Yes, that's like a primer in Hermetic Alchemy, " said Antanov, " but I think even Eco himself was conflicted when he wrote the story."

"Hermetic Alchemy?" said Bigsy, " That's a bit of a rich one for this time in the morning."

"Let's start with the rose, " said Antanov. Most Freemasons are on the lookout for symbols, so Christina showing up with an acacia - sign of innocence, but then a rose - powerful alchemy and a Triangle - which normally contains the Supreme Being's ever watchful eye. It'd blow their minds."

"And I thought it was the von Fürstenberg!" said Christina.

"Mmm. Nice, " said Clare approvingly.

"Well the rose, " said Antanov, " It has three tiers of petals. The first tier, of three petals, represents the three basic alchemical elements: salt, mercury, and sulphur.

"The tier of seven petals represents the seven Classical planets

"The tier of twelve represents the astrological zodiac. Each of the twenty-two petals bears one of the twenty-two letters in the Hebrew alphabet and also represents the twenty-two paths on the Tree of Life.

"It's shaky pseudo-science then, " said Bigsy. "I thought petals followed a Fibonacci series. And anyway, most roses have a five-petal centre?"

"Come to think of it the planets number is a bit off too. Some artful thinking here?"

"Bigsy, when was the last time you've given a bouquet to a love of your life? - Give the man a break, " said Jake laughing.

"Okay, I agree, the whole premise may have some flaws, but plenty of people will follow its direction in any case, " said Antanov, "And it meant Christina was flaunting an attitude to those Freemasons."

"And then we get to the Rosicrucians themselves. Rosicrucianism is a spiritual and cultural movement which arose in Europe in the early 17th century after the publication of several texts which purported to announce the existence of a hitherto unknown esoteric order to the world and made seeking its knowledge attractive to many.

"Christina turning up at the Lodge signalling herself as an Adept of the Rosicrucian order will have blown some of their first-degree minds. Being clad in that blue gown adds another dimension too. There's a thing called the Blue Lodge, which only the top Masons can attend. There isn't even one in the UK anywhere, so it has a kind of mythical status. Think about it, 'A woman from the Blue Lodge, an adept Rosicrucian' - it's off the symbolic scale.'

"The Rosicrucian manifestos heralded a 'universal reformation of mankind', through a science allegedly kept secret for decades until the intellectual climate might receive it.

"Some sort of fake news included though, " said Bigsy.

Antanov continues, " Hmm, yes, controversies arose on whether they were a hoax, whether the 'Order of the Rosy Cross' existed as described in the manifestos, and whether the whole thing was a metaphor disguising a movement that really existed, but in a different form.

"The mysterious doctrine of the order is 'built on esoteric truths of the ancient past', which 'concealed from the average man, provide insight into nature, the physical universe, and the spiritual realm'."

"Wow; it almost sound primordial, " Said Bigsy.

"Yes, it is supposed to, " answered Antanov, " That's part of its power - and you can see how it could be sealed hermetically inside a monastery, like in that Alberto Eco story."

"Or exploited cynically, by some opportunistic financiers?" added Clare.

"Antanov, I'm so glad you didn't tell me all of this before. It's a lot to comprehend, " said Christina.

"I would have, but we didn't really have lot of time and then that ebullient woman adding the sprig of acacia meant symbolism overload. You were really signposted like Alpha to Omega. Innocent to Adept."

"So, is that why I had so many men come over to say hello?" asked Christina.

"Er, I think that might have been because we were on the same table as Nathalie and her blonde friend, Nina" said Antanov.

"Oh yes, the ones arranged by Jennifer Sussex - I just remembered her name - Nathalie told me it when we were in the washroom."

"Useful, " said Jake, " There's another line to follow. We might be able to work out how often these events take place."

"So, is this moving us along?" asked Clare.

"I think so, " said Jake, " Look, we now know who sponsored the session, at least one of the people being influenced. We know who is doing the lobbying and the means being used. Plus, we've external leads to follow up. The office by the Dome and some sort of contact with Bernard Driscoll."

"You know who could help with that last point? - Amanda Miller." Said Bigsy, " And I think that is how Chuck got the address in Germany that we followed."

Mystery address at the dome

Bigsy and Christina took the Jubilee Line to Canada Water. They emerged from the long escalator to a courtyard that led in a semicircle towards the Dome.

"Many's the time I've been here to see music acts, " said Bigsy, " Although sometimes they can be little dots in the distance."

"Sometimes the gigs are in the smaller venue, " said Christina, switching into muso mode for a few seconds.

"Oh yes, I suppose you know all about venues and their capacity from 'living the dream', " said Bigsy, " We'll need to turn to the right here, "

They branched off towards some colourful plate glass buildings which seemed to be arranged along the bank of the Thames.

"Now remember, we are here for an interview, " said Bigsy.

They looked again at the address and checked the floor. It was to be the 6th floor of the building.

Their meeting was entirely fictitious, but they thought it might get them through the first stage of the building security.

They entered through the revolving doors. Christina quickly scoped the layout. Reception to the left, turnstiles central, no separate access for the lifts. Excellent."

"Hello, we are here to visit Recognition Consultants, we are from Bluefish Recruitment. We have a meeting with the head of HR."

"Okay that's Janie Parker, just one moment."

He dialled a number. "Voicemail, " he muttered.

"Okay, I think Ms Parker said if she was not available then to go to speak to one of her staff."

"Let me try again, " He dialled again, " Oh, Hello, I've two people here to see Janie Parker, they are from Bluefish Recruitment…Okay…I'll check…Yes…Right…Ring you again…Okay…Yes…Okay."

"They will see you in a moment. Here, let me make the badges. They will get you in and out today only. Please hand them back to one of the security people when you leave. Please look at the Blue square on the wall. Thank you. And now you, Sir, Thank you."

They completed the rest of their details and were each handed a lanyard.

"Please put this around your neck and keep the badge visible. The orange denotes visitor."

"You can go on through now, to the Sixth floor. Tap it in the elevator. Someone will meet you at the doors."

"Excellent, " said Christina to Bigsy. "We are in."

They were met at the Sixth floor.

"Hello, I'm Petra, Janie isn't available at the moment, but I can probably help you."

She showed them through to a glass sided meeting room.

"Look, I haven't booked this one, so we might get kicked out at half past. People just book these rooms and then don't turn up to use them."

"Coffee, or water?"

"A coffee would be lovely, " said Christina.

"I'm good, " said Bigsy.

"Okay, it'll be machine - you don't mind? - I'll just go outside to fetch some."

"I'll come with you, " said Christina.

They left Bigsy alone in the office. He wandered out through the door. In front was a wall of filing cupboards, there was an occasional gap which served the function of door access to the clusters of pods. He noticed they were packed pretty tight, much like call-centre. Everyone he could see had a headset, with a microphone. This was a call-centre. He noticed a couple of supervisor booths in the corner of the office. Slightly higher flooring and a glass side, like the meeting room, so that the supervisor could look out.

He noticed Christina and Petra returning.

"Now what can I help you with today?" asked Petra.

"Well, that's just it, " said Christina, " Ms Parker invited us in for a talk about requirements, I think she said you were hiring?"

"Em, this is quite embarrassing, " said Petra, " But I'm not sure I know what this is about."

"That's okay, " said Christina, " We flew in from Amsterdam this morning, but we have meetings with a couple of other clients as well, *Hey Dave, je controleert je afspraken voor later, nietwaar?*"

Bigsy looked confused and said, " Yes, later today we've more appointments."

Christina was calling him by his real first name - very formal.

"I'm afraid this might all be a visit in vain, today, " said Petra.

"Okay, no worries, although perhaps you'd give us the tuppenny tour of the floor on the way out, for future reference."

"Why certainly, " said Petra.

"As you can see, we are an American organisation, Consultancy, but we field a lot of direct enquiries from here in this call-centre. They can be direct from clients or passed on via our field representatives."

"It sounds like it is multi-lingual too, " said Christina, " That's probably why you contacted us. We couldn't use the name babel fish, but Bluefish consultants deals with many languages too."

"I can see the little flags now, this must be the Scandinavian section, there's Norway, Sweden and -er - Denmark?"

"That's right, " said Petra, clearly a little confused by flags and the languages being spoken.

Bigsy held out his phone and quietly took a couple of pictures. He noticed the number of American accents talking as well as the multiple languages. The large screens in the room were running US television too, no sound but subtitles. Each set of cubicles has a cluster of TVs showing a mix of Fox, CBS, NBC, BBC America, Bloomberg and CNN.

He also looked at the desk clutter, there he noticed a lanyard and a badge. Blue circle, white shield, red compass, white eagle's head. It could only be one thing.

CIA.

Now they were back at the lifts.

"Here we are, " said Petra, " Back at the elevators, don't forget its G for ground not 1, " she showed them through the doors, they waited a few seconds and then the lifts appeared.

"Well, I'm real sorry for your trouble today, " said Petra.

"Not at all, " said Christina, " And thank you for the refreshment."

They climbed into the lift.

Christina pressed G. Bigsy then pressed 5.

They looked at one another as the lift started to descend.

"I'm going to take one more swift look, " he said, " Please take my jacket."

They arrived at 5 and then he pressed 6 again. The was going to go to the ground before starting its ascent.

At the Sixth floor he came out of the lift. Instead of turning left, he took the doors to the right. He wondered whether his lanyard badge would open the door to the floor. It did and he walked in. It looked like a mirror image of the area he'd visited earlier.

He walked through the cubicle areas to one which looked more lightly populated. Then he walked along the rows of seats to one with a jacket on the back of the chair. He put it on and was walking out.

"Hey, who are you - that's Jim's jacket, " called an American voice.

"Oh, this is so embarrassing, I can tell now that this isn't my jacket. I've lost mine and was about to go to a meeting. All these cubicles look the same. Is this the north side of the building?

"Take a look out of the window, Bud, what can you see? - No River eh? No, you are southside. You need to cut through those double doors and across to the other side. You'd better put Jim's jacket back though. Don't worry, we've all got lost at some time or other in this place."

The questioner smiled towards Bigsy as he very carefully placed the jacket over the seat.

"Thanks for your help, " said Bigsy as he made his way back to the double doors.

Christina was waiting downstairs when Bigsy arrived.

"What happened? She asked, " I got lost, " said Bigsy. They both beeped their way past the turnstile and then handed their lanyards and badge in to a security guard.

Outside, the sun was shining, they walked back towards the tube.

"Well?" asked Christina.

"Definitely American, " said Bigsy, " Some kind of monitoring operation, judging by the screens on the desks. I got this."

He fished into his trouser pocket.

He pulled out a badge, 'Anne-Marie Bristow', it said, CIA Field Agent, " I had to grab it from a desk as I walked past. I nearly got caught." Said Bigsy, " Curious, though, I was expecting it to be a Russian setup."

"Yes, that's what they are doing. The Americans are laying a false trail to the Russians for what they have been doing around Raven, " said Christina, " It would also explain why Blackbird knows nothing about this. I'll probably need to report this in - or get Antanov to."

"I suppose they can monitor finance systems from here, quite well."

"They have a clear look at the London flightpath to Heathrow too, this could be an excellent location for a listening post, " said Christina. She was thinking back to her father's listening station built into the wool store when they lived in Iceland.

Chuck

Mud can make you prisoner,
and the plains can bake you dry
Snow can burn your eyes,
but only people make you cry
Home is made for comin' from,
for dreams of goin' to
Which with any luck will never come true
I was born under a wandrin' star
I was born under a wandrin' star

Alan Jay Lerner / Frederick Loewe

'Bin a long time

They were in the Triangle's offices, sat around a table.

"So now we really do need Chuck, to help us get to the bottom of what is happening over in Canada Water, " said Clare

"That is okay then, " said Jake, " Chuck is due to be here today. He'll finally meet Christina too, and we can reset things onto an even keel."

"And then we can ask Chuck what he knows about CIA in East London, " said Clare.

At that moment, Chuck entered the office. He was on his cell phone. He hung up and turned to the group.

"Hello, I'm Chuck," he said warmly, " but I don't think I've met you before?"

"I'm Christina, " said Christina, " Very pleased to meet you. I have heard so much about you." She stood as if to shake his hand.

"Hi Christina, Katarina Voronin, and various other

names. Your reputation precedes you. I'm fascinated to meet you." said Chuck, " And I guess this office and work with "The Triangle" should be considered neutral? – See I can follow Jake's instructions!"

"Agreed, " said Christina, " I hear you can be pretty lethal too, with a SAM or two. I think there's probably enough to do here without worrying about one another."

Chuck held out his hand and Christina delicately shook it.

"Accord, " said Jake.

"Glastnost and Perestroika, " said Chuck.

"Prozrachnost' restrukturizatsii i mira, " said Christina, " Transparency, Restructuring and Peace."

Clare laughed, " We'll all drink to that."

"So, what have you discovered?" asked Chuck, " Something about an American Station in Canada Water?"

"Yes, we think we stumbled on a listening station, but the strange thing was that the American agents there were pretending to be Russian."

"We'll, they were pretending to be Russian to the outside world, but inside there were Americans and some hired help that was operating as multiple nationalities."

"Okay, I'll have a dig around, but what would this have to do with Raven?"

"We are not certain, although it seems that a German outfit might be implicated: ISMC, "

"And more, we think Bernard Driscoll, you know, the MP and Minister, might be being used as an unwitting influencer in all of this."

"Hold on, ISMC isn't German, we've had dealings, " said Chuck, " It is based in London."

"It makes sense, said Christina, the guy I was talking too, Gerhardt Schmidt, might have been bragging about his own importance. He was from Germany and said that was where the company was based."

"Unreliable source, I'm afraid, I think there are some UK top brass fronting up ISMC, " said Chuck.

"Sir Charles Frobisher, by any chance?" asked Christina.

"No idea, " said Chuck, " I don't really follow who is who in the corporate side of things. I'm more of a 'hands-on' kind of guy."

"Well, let's see what we can find out, is there someone you can ask?" asked Clare.

"Not directly, I should go through my channels, but don't you see what that would do? If our CIA is running an operation to tip a country towards America, they won't appreciate my little questions getting in the way."

"It must be the same for you, Christina? If Russia is getting twitchy about what Raven is trying to do then a Russian agent probing around in the mix is going to cause ructions. I think we are reaching a stalemate."

Christina was looking thoughtful, " What about if we use another power to intervene in this? One option would be the mysterious forces of the Freemasons, but another would be the Brits. After all, most of this is happening on their soil right now. Raven, Masons, ISMC, Frobisher, Driscoll. All being used to tip the scales."

"Yes, and remember what Nelson's friend Jeval said, It seems to be about oil rights in Celarus. Who would ever suspect the UK of manipulation in such a situation?"

"Can we contact SI6? Amanda Miller? We had quite some dealings with her back in the case of the toxins and the London bomb outside of the Bank of England."

"Ahem, I might just have a good contact with Amanda at the moment, " spluttered Chuck, looking unusually bashful.

"Chuck?" asked Clare, " Nooo? Are you and Amanda - er -friendly?"

"In a manner of speaking, we had an enjoyable dinner last week in J Sheekey's, as it happens. Well, I was in town and called her up. That phone number identity that Jake requested."

"J Sheekey's is an awfully big 'thank you' for a phone number Chuck, " said Clare.

"Let's say I wanted to see Amanda...Look can we move on, "

Christina and Clare looked at one another, they could see that Chuck was quietly squirming.

"Okay, so let's figure this out, how do we best describe this to Amanda?" asked Christina.

Clare continued, " Well, we know that Amanda doesn't think much of Driscoll. She seems to think he's full of self-importance and puffery, has little respect for others and pretends to always know what is best for everyone. As I describe this, I realise that she is right."

"So that would make some interesting incentive for her to get involved in this?" asked Bigsy.

"You bet, " said Clare.

"The weirdest dynamic is that we are right in the middle of a political situation though. Celarus aided and abetted by the Americans to get out from under Russia. This could cut up rough for Christina and Antanov, "

"Trust us, we've both had jams like this before, " said Christina, " and situations where we were asked to act but we didn't even know the moves being made."

"Okay then, we'll ask Amanda for help. She can check up on Driscoll and may even be able to find out some more about that American station on the Thames."

"Who is going to ask her?" They all looked towards Chuck.

"Er, I guess that's going to be me then."

"Good luck, " said Clare.

Fake News

Amanda received the call from Chuck. She couldn't help wondering if it had been planned, although Chuck protested most strongly that this had all come along since she'd found him that phone number in Germany.

It was an elaborate example of follow the dots.

Chuck had told her two pieces of news. About Driscoll and about the American Station in Canada Water.

He had not needed to tell her about the second item, so she guessed he must have been feeling particularly sheepish about how things had played out. Anyway, she would treat the American Station with some caution as she started to investigate. Of course, she already knew about it, but the American station was really annoying her.

She knew the Americans had moved their operations to the South side of the river, when they set up shop in Nine Elms. And just because they had a friendly sounding ambassador with a name like 'Woody' didn't mean that Yael, Elizabeth and Susan wouldn't get up to something.

She supposed the Americans were following their

Grosvenor Square playbook. For years the gilded aluminium bald eagle on the roof of the Chancery building had made it a landmark, but also pulled eyes away from the myriad of smaller satellite buildings quietly going about America's work.

Ever since the Americans sold the original building with its underground labyrinth to the Qataris, it was to become the finest spy hotel in London., right in the middle of the diplomatic area. Property developer Trump had said the Americans had got a bad deal, but he'd done nothing to intervene.

Instead, the Americans now had a moated building with some pleasant gardens away from the normal protest areas of London, yes still within listening device distance of the Houses of Parliament and the Cabinet Offices. Maybe not at the peppercorn rent from the Duke of Westminster, but who is counting?

Amanda had long understood the Americans wanting another listening station to cover East London too. It was not so far from the financial sector in Canary Wharf, literally one stop on the strategic Jubilee line. And it could also probe into the emerging area of New Chinatown, being developed along by the Victoria Docks and the City Airport.

Amanda had put in a similar request for SI6 premises along that stretch of river but had been told to wait until the Chinese developments were further along. It was like kicking her plans into the long grass. But what bugged her was that somehow the Americans had got away with doing what she had planned - and in her own home city.

As for Bernard Driscoll, she remembered her dealings with this blustering politician. Bullying, lying, feeble minded, yet his reassuring haughtiness seemed to convince the public that he knew what he was doing when he clearly had no idea. He always seemed to be shored up by some of the tabloid press.

What was worse was that he seemed to convince himself. Amanda wondered whether he was also being operated by someone else.

A few days ago, he had been in the Commons to give what came billed as an "urgent statement on defence measures following our change of status".

He wouldn't directly confront issues either - we would have to guess whether he was talking about post-Brexit, an oil situation or a possible financial meltdown.

No end of probing by interviewers would deflect his path either. It was recognised among the media that this was not Driscoll being clever, but that he was mentally challenged and rather thick-skinned.

A standard speech by him usually included one of his greatest hits' statements: "We haven't got everything right" he would concede as an afterthought – a bit of humility never goes amiss – but by and large he couldn't think of a thing he would have done differently.

Whole streams of questions could be fired at him, but because of his status as the Minister for External Affairs, he could parry most of them with puffery.

His Ministry was well provisioned by the Official Secrets Act, meaning we may find out about his position in 30 years' time, but Driscoll was at his most Uriah Heep in his other answers.

Even on hard facts like statistics, he would wriggle and bend the truth. Numbers of troops, status of preparedness, strategic alliances.

With his way with arithmetic, where every finger and thumb could have been counted separately let alone shoes and boots, such that we could have as many boots on the ground in any territory that he deemed significant. Fake News spun here.

He'd been investigated on Panorama too, for a couple of situations where the UK had sold armaments and munitions to unusual foreign powers. It always seemed curious that his name would be in there somewhere greasing the wheels of commerce. No, he could not take credit for any of these situations.

Bernard's ears always pricked up at the suggestion of any admission of wrongdoing. He had been in politics long enough not to implicate himself in anything that might have legal liability when a public inquiry is an inevitability.

He could wheel out scientists or experts, just as well as Tony Blair did. He was always working to the scientist or military advisor specification. That the hitherto unknown advisory group SMIG Scientific Military Intelligence Group had been all over his plans. It didn't tally with anything heard previously. Amanda had cross checked the SMIG files but found them embarrassingly empty; apparently the Group had been retro fitted onto another one that discussed tracked vehicle rights of access to sites of scientific interest. Another false underpinning.

No journalist had bothered to dig that far, and Driscoll had got it all blocked with redactions, Secrets Act and

Top Secrets classifications. All of which could be quickly dismantled to help the scientists be lined up for a show trial if and when the dust finally settled.

Amanda knew she would need to approach Driscoll but was ready, once again, for his veneer of civility masking condescension and contempt.

She knew, that whatever she said to him, he wasn't going to apologise for anything. Why should he? If he was going down, he would be making sure to take as many of his colleagues with him and particularly any already identified as potential fall-guys.

Yes, Driscoll, with his surrounding bubble of corporate advisors would think himself invincible.

Excuse

Amanda had called Bernard Driscoll's office and set the agenda for a meeting. She had said that it had come to light that a new 'fake sheik' was doing the rounds and that he needed to be aware of the implications.

Driscoll had responded well to this, particularly because Amanda made it seem as if another Minister had already been caught out. Amanda knew he would want to feed on the gossip from such a situation and look for any angles where he could bury a potential rival.

She was waiting in Driscoll's outer office in Portcullis House. She had been there thirty minutes. She remembered that Driscoll liked to convey an impression of importance by being busy.

Sure, enough at 31 minutes after the booked time, she was let in to see him.

She opened the door to his office. He appeared to be on the telephone.

"Yes…Yes…Possibly…That's settled then, " he hung up.

"Ah Amanda, how good of you to come over, " he

treacled with a schoolmaster tone.

She remembered that he also delighted in getting people to come to him, rather than to go out. Unless it was to somewhere thoroughly agreeable.

"Hello Bernard, I thought we should catch up, I've some potentially disturbing news for you, especially given your role in export of defence equipment."

Driscoll sat upon the defence export marketplace, which positioned the UK as the world's second biggest defence exporter over the last decade, selling about $122bn (£98bn) of equipment of which 63% of its defence exports were sold to the Middle East.

"You'll have noticed that someone is using a series of written parliamentary questions to uncover the statistics of the sales, " said Amanda.

"That the person is part of a TV production team looking into allegations of bribery and corruption and that sufficient action has not been taken to ensure that the UK's defence sales are held to the highest standards, " she continued.

"Piffle, " said Driscoll, " Balderdash and piffle."

Amanda noticed the new vocabulary which became prevalent in the current Parliament. Very public-school framed.

She continued, " They say they do not believe that the UK government should permit weapons sales to regimes such as Saudi Arabia which use them against civilians, but if they do so, then they must at the very least ensure that UK taxpayers' money is not spent on bribing foreign officials who are part of corrupt regimes."

Driscoll started one of his speeches, " For the UK to fail to uphold standards on corruption and transparency erodes both our good reputation abroad and our ability to be a positive influence around the world."

"Our interactions with other countries should prioritise human rights and the public good, which does not involve bribing dubious regimes to buy weapons from us which they will then use in contravention of international law."

"Look Amanda, this is old news. The Ministry of Defence has already rebutted these allegations. They said that they took allegations of fraud, theft, corruption and bribery seriously and worked hard to detect and deter it. I think they went on to say that there were robust processes in place to raise awareness of the need for vigilance and MoD actively encourage individuals to report any of these acts. To be like whistle-blowers."

Amanda continued, " Well, we both know that the MoD routinely carries out checks on potential contractors prior to contract award, including on criminal activity, such as convictions for tax evasion, bribery or fraud, and a review of a company's audited accounts. "

"Yes, " said Driscoll, " Then the Cabinet Office coordinates procurement of public sector contracts and says it has made the process more open and transparent, becoming the first G7 country to commit to standards that will ensure every part of the process is visible to the public."

"I think we can say that the UK Government is committed to be the most transparent government in the world."

Amanda thought to herself, " He'll be using that line in interviews next."

Amanda said, " So it would take a Deep State conspiracy to provision arms to somewhere less desirable then, and there's no hint of bribery or corruption."

"None whatsoever, " said Driscoll, " I hope that puts your mind at rest."

"I guess I'm paid to worry about these things, " said Amanda, " And to warn Ministers when I see trouble looming."

"Not this time, " said Driscoll, " I think you've wasted your trip from Vauxhall Cross. You can tell your experts there that they are barking up the wrong tree. Was there anything else, or are we finished?"

Amanda noticed a programme for Formula One tossed onto Driscoll's desk.

"No, that's all I think, at least I feel better now I've raised the flag about this."

"Well, goodbye, then, Ms Miller. Audrey will show you out."

A suited woman appeared, and ushered Amanda from the room. "That's a lovely brooch, " she said to Audrey, noticing the small golden emblem on Audrey's lapel. Amanda noticed it seemed to be like sprig of some kind of tree.

"Thank you- it is pretty, my husband gave it to me, "

Audrey replied, " Do you know your way from here?"

"Oh yes," said Amanda, "Many's the time I've walked this corridor!"

Amanda calls Chuck

Amanda was back close to her office in Vauxhall. She was on the bank of the River Thames, sitting on a bench. She called Chuck.

"Hi Amanda, I guess you can talk now?"

"Hi Chuck, yes, I'm away from my desk', " she said.

"Got it, so did you find out anything?"

"Not so much. Driscoll is even more infuriating than I remembered him. He wasn't in the least bit interested in my warning about a corruption investigation. He said it was all old news and that he had it all covered. Something I noticed, though, was that his assistant is an interesting form of gatekeeper. I noticed that she had a small brooch, which I think was Masonic. She said it was a present from her husband, so that might be a lead in itself.

"You think Driscoll's assistant has a link to the Freemasons?"

"Could be, and as a woman she'd be beyond suspicion."

"What was their chemistry like?"

"Brisk, I'd say, business-like. I doubt whether Driscoll would ever recognise that he was being played."

"And nothing leading about new developments?"

"No, I wonder whether Driscoll is clever enough to cover it up, or whether he simply doesn't know at the moment."

"Okay, thank you Amanda, I do appreciate this; would you like to stay involved?"

"I would if you think it leads to something, or maybe if I can assist again, otherwise I've plenty of other situations that we are handling right now. I've got to go to Cheltenham tomorrow about one of the situations."

"Okay, but I hope you'll keep some time in your calendar for me?" asked Chuck.

"I think I might be able to manage that, " said Amanda, smiling.

Acacia

Chuck was back in the Triangle offices with Christina, Jake and Clare.

"I thought I'd bring you up to date, following Amanda's visits to Driscoll. There was nothing obvious that she could find. Driscoll is slippery at the best of times and on the thought of an implied corruption he was reaching for the scapegoats."

Amanda told me about Driscoll's assistant too. She was wearing a golden brooch like a sprig from a bush or tree. I always thought that was a Chinese lucky symbol, but Amanda wondered if it was Masonic."

"Leaves" queried Christina, " Are you sure it wasn't an acacia bush? Let me show you."

She dived into her purse and found the Freemason brooch from Raven.

"Can I photograph it?" asked Chuck, who snapped it to his phone and then tapped in something else.

"I've sent it to Amanda, " he said, " Let's see if she identifies it."

As he said that, there was a ping on his phone.

"Wow, she must like you a lot!" said Christina.

Chuck replied, " Yes - It's the same as the one that Amanda saw. Driscoll has a Freemason assistant. Well, a woman who knows a Freemason, at least."

PART TWO

When we all fall asleep, where do we go?

*White shirt now red, my bloody nose
Sleepin', you're on your tippy toes
Creepin' around like no one knows
Think you're so criminal
Bruises on both my knees for you
Don't say thank you or please
I do what I want when I'm wanting to
My soul? So cynical*

Billie Eilish Pirate Baird O'Connell

Iraq news report

IRAQ [INR-01278AP] Based upon recent media reports: A vehicle convoy of 12 Raven trucks (civilian contractors) and a security element consisting of five Humvees departed from LSA Python en route to Forward Operating Base McKlusky. The Humvees belonged to the Transportation Company of the 207th Battalion of the Corps Support Group.

During the mission, inaccurate map data caused the convoy commander to make a wrong turn and led the convoy into an ambush with small arms fire, rocket-propelled grenades and hand grenades. Unfortunately, three civilians employed by the Raven subsidiary Qube were killed during the attack. Three other Qube civilian employees and one Soldier were also wounded.

Immediately following the attack, the Corps Support Group based at LSA Python conducted an investigation into the incident.

The investigation determined military personnel responded properly to events on the ground and did not abandon the convoy as it came under attack. Although the convoy commander conducted thorough pre-combat inspections and checks in accordance with standard operating procedures, the investigation report recommended that convoy rehearsals be more comprehensive in the future.

During the course of the ambush with small arms fire, RPGs and hand grenades, gun trucks continued to lay suppressive fire and several of the Qube drivers were wounded and their vehicles disabled. At one point during the ambush, the convoy commander ordered his vehicle to move forward and assist the Qube personnel in the lead convoy vehicles that were disabled and under fire. This was likely the gun truck pictured in a video provided to the media by a Raven employee who was injured during the ambush.

Multi-National Force-Iraq officials said although they have not seen the video in its entirety, it appears that the gun truck moving forward in the video was not fleeing the kill zone but instead was moving to contact the disabled Qube trucks in front of it (outside the camera angle). This gun truck stopped at those Qube trucks and laid down fire; eventually it proceeded out of the kill zone to the rally point established by the lead gun truck, calling in close air support, a quick reaction force and medical evacuations en route and later preparing a landing zone for the inbound medevac helicopter.

The other gun trucks (in the rear of the convoy) remained in the area directly behind and continued to return suppressive fire. A combination of those escort military gun trucks and Qube vehicles moved up the line of Qube vehicles rescuing drivers in two vehicles. Attack aviation helicopters responded to the attack, and the quick reaction force arrived within approximately 30 minutes to repel the insurgents. Two individuals were medically evacuated from the scene.

MNF-I officials said the actions of the Transportation Company saved numerous lives during this attack, and at no time did U.S. military personnel abandon the convoy. The Transportation Company bravely returned fire and protected the convoy while waiting for reinforcements and attending to casualties. U.S. military personnel, as well as Qube truck drivers, demonstrated valor and level-headedness during the attack. Their actions were honorable and should not be depicted otherwise. The investigation recognized the noble actions of one Soldier and one civilian and recommended they be submitted for awards commensurate with their actions.

Despite the valiant actions of the Transportation Company, three Qube civilian employees lost their lives. MNF-I officials said civilian contractors are a vital part of Coalition efforts to develop a peaceful and democratic Iraq, and the MNF-I deeply regret their loss.

Burghers

Amanda looked at the report. It would normally be routine, but on this occasion, she noticed it because it mentioned Raven and their subsidiary Qube, caught up in a firefight in Iraq.

She selected the report text and pasted it across into her notepad. There were no security markings. She guessed this was because the report was trying to clear the US Army from an accusation of not protecting a civilian convoy on its way to a forward position.

She would have to tell Chuck of this situation, it looked pertinent to the situation with Driscoll and Raven.

"Meet in Victoria Tower Gardens" she texted. "By the Burghers."

"Ha ha, " came a reply from Chuck, " Give me one hour, please, "

She checked her watch. She could easily walk there in an hour, but she had no idea where Chuck was travelling from.

After half an hour she decided to set off and realised that she would be in the Victoria Gardens in about ten minutes. Another ten to reach the statue so she would have ten minutes to look at one of Rodin's masterpieces.

Amanda knew that 'Les Bourgeois de Calais' commemorates an event during the Hundred Years' War, when Calais was under siege by the English for about eleven months. Calais commissioned Rodin to create the sculpture.

King Edward offered to spare the people of the city if six of its leaders would surrender themselves to him, presumably to be executed. Edward demanded that they walk out wearing nooses around their necks and carrying the keys to the city and castle.

One of the wealthiest of the town leaders, Eustache de Saint Pierre, volunteered first, and five other burghers joined with him. The six Burghers of Calais.

Saint Pierre led this envoy of volunteers to the city gates. It was this moment, and this poignant mix of defeat, heroic self-sacrifice, and willingness to face imminent death that Rodin captured in his sculpture, scaled somewhat larger than life.

The burghers expected to be executed, but their lives were spared by the intervention of England's queen, Philippa of Hainault, who persuaded her husband to exercise mercy by claiming that their deaths would be a bad omen for her unborn child.

"But was it real, or political theatre?" asked Chuck, smiling as he approached. They kissed, and Amanda felt like a naughty schoolgirl on a secret assignation, rather than the head of a major UK secrets unit.

"We ought really to be more careful, " she said, " With you a foreign agent and all."

"But have you declared me to the people inside?" asked Chuck.

"You know, I ought to, but I just haven't got around to it yet. I wasn't sure if we were 'a thing'.

"Wasn't sure! wasn't sure?" smiled Chuck, " Well I think I know…however awkward this gets in the manuals and HR departments!"

"So, what did you find out?"

Amanda showed Chuck her note from her phone's notepad.

"This is very useful, " said Chuck, " We can use this event creatively to shake the tree, "

"That's what I wondered, " said Amanda, " Although it might call for a combined operation."

"Let me take this to the guys in the Triangle, it's not got any confidentiality markings, has it? - Can we air share it, please?

"Certainly, and it is obvious they wanted this to get out

onto the wires, " answered Amanda, she pressed some keys on her phone and the image transferred to Chuck's phone.

"Excellent, and how about tomorrow evening, I could report back to you from a lovely relaxed setting?"

"Mondrian?" asked Amanda, " How could I refuse!"

Time for Stetsons?

Chuck arrived at the Triangle offices.

"What? Three days in a row? We are indeed honoured!" quipped Bigsy.

"I've something of interest, " said Chuck, " A report of a skirmish. In Iraq, it included Raven and Qube contractors. Sadly some casualties."

Chuck beamed the memo to their wall projector. It was sideways.

"Wiggle your phone to turn it around, " suggested Bigsy.

"I'm all over this technology, " said Chuck, instead clicking a couple of controls on the screen. The image rotated and they all started to read it. Bigsy snapped it onto his phone as well.

"I was thinking of a visit, " said Chuck, " to Raven's main Headquarters."

"Been there, " said Bigsy.

"No, not their Head Office, their main HQ in the USA."

"Where's that?" asked Clare.

"In Austin, Texas, " said Chuck.

"Austin!" said Clare, " I've been there - actually Christina and I were there together for SWSX a couple of years ago. Christina had a gig in Maggie Mae's; it was rammed."

"Yes, that whole Sixth Street music scene is pretty lively, " agreed Christina. Just lucky we both had Stetsons and boots for that particular evening."

"And the street was full of people, bobbing from club to club. Sixth Street nights, eh!"

"Well, this seems to be a Headquarters building in an altogether more corporate campus part of Austin."

"So how are we going to play this?" asked Bigsy.

"I think we'll use some investigative journalism. What happened on that mission? What's the link to Raven, to Qube? I feel this one might be good for any journalists we might have amongst us?"

Everyone looked towards Jake. Journalism had been his main employment right up to the start of The Triangle and it had got him into the mischief that led to them being able to fund the Triangle.

"Okay, count me in, " said Jake, " Will you go too?" asked Jake, looking towards Chuck.

"Tricky, " said Chuck. "I think I'd set off all kinds of alerts at Homeland Security when we entered the USA. If I'm going back innocuously then it's okay, but when I'm on a mission, not such a good idea."

"Okay, who then? I think you may need to be able to handle yourselves in a scrape. I'd recommend Christina as the most likely, " said Chuck.

Christina looked up, " Sure, although - ahem - I've still got Antanov staying with me now. I said he could stay while he was in London."

"Okay, but I think this will be a short trip, in any case, " said Chuck. "Visit Raven, ask questions, return."

"That's the thing, " said Jake, " Normally we'd do this kind of short sharp thing by conference call."

"Not if we are taking photographs as well, " said Christina, " You forget, I was also photographer in Paris."

They looked at Christina. "I had to give it up, people kept wanting me to take pictures for them."

"Great, " said Chuck., " We have a plan., " Christina and Jake to visit Raven, for an independent voice of truth investigative journal in the UK. Jake to run interviews, Christina to take photographs and both of them to snoop around."

"Okay, we'll need a magazine title or something, " said Jake, " Not one of Bigsy's made up web pages, but a real one. Ideally something that brings in guest journalists, sometimes anonymously. - I'm thinking Spectator."

"Ew, " said Clare, " That's tricky to impersonate and I think they'd be quite annoyed if they found out."

"Yes, but they love the USA and are all for close ties. They even have an American edition; Let's remind ourselves that Boris Johnson wrote for them as well as a few Cabinet Ministers."

"We can modify what we say, that we are freelance but planning our article for publication in the Spectator."

"That works, " said Jake, " and gives us some wriggle room. Now we need to get the interview."

"Assumptive close, " said Clare, " We imply that its already been agreed and we are just tidying up the loose end arrangements."

"Let's find their Board, " said Bigsy looking through the internet, " Here we are, how high do we want to go?"

He flicked the list of Corporate Officers onto the screen.

"Skip over the CEO and Head of Global Business Lines; we'd need someone like HR Officer for a realistic interview. They might also want to bring along a General Counsel, " Said Jake.

"Okay, " said Clare, " I've got a couple of names here: Mark McKown and Mary Spalding, Let's see what I can make happen. I'll go into the quiet room, if that's okay with everyone."

Clare lifted her laptop and set off for another office, one that Bigsy had soundproofed, but which they had discovered was also ideal for making phone calls.

"If anyone can get us the meeting, then it'll be Clare, " said Bigsy, " Her PR skills and contacts are second to none."

Texas

I learned to drive on those East Texas red clay backroads
And I mean to tell you my friend
They weren't no easy roads
You had to watch out for all the curves
Down by Kelsey Creek
And detour through the Lindsay's pasture
When the water ran too deep

Michelle Shocked

I'll need to get a bigger camera

"It is done, " said Clare, triumphantly. "Raven's PR actually said they were hoping that someone would bite at that newswire listing. There were accusations about the US military running scared at that ambush, but DoD, Raven and Qube all want to refute that story. They say that the Press Release was an attempt to do so, but they would welcome any more in-depth investigations to reposition the story.

"Their PR is going to get us a senior member of their HR team, plus, as we suspected someone from Legal Counsel and one of the Qube employees involved in the ambush. They asked, Christina, whether you'd prefer the employee to be in their desert gear, rather than a suit, for the photographs. They also said they would try to arrange for a Qube truck to be available for the day, for some photographs.

"Clare, that's outstanding, " said Chuck, delighted with what he was hearing.

Clare continued, " They also saw the need for speed on this story, before it melts away into the background. I went along with this and so I've arranged the shoot and interview for Friday."

"Friday this week! We'd better get moving." said Jake.

"I'll also need a bigger camera, " said Christina. "One that looks more impressive to the client."

"Let's hire some gear then, " said Bigsy, " We can go comprehensive that way and it will look well-used."

"Good idea, " said Christina, " Portrait lenses, something wide angle to capture the truck. Some LED lights. A wheeled case to transport it all."

Frozen Margaritas machine

Christina was sitting next to Jake on the plane, they had been pleasantly chatting and watching movies. Then the movies suddenly came to a halt.

"They always do that, " said Jake, " Now I'll have to watch the whole film again."

"Was it any good?" asked Christina, " This Jane Austen adaptation seemed fairly good. Emma's rich girl hobby is manipulative match-making, but she's not particularly good at it, nor at her own attempts at romance."

"Your one seems to have a lot of flashing violence on the screen?"

"Yeah, it's one of the Marvel characters, who has a bust up with the Joker and then blows up a chemical plant, I'm pretty sure there's more sassy mayhem to follow, " said Jake, " But I'll have to download it."

They both looked around the plane. The air stewards were in the early stages of preparing for a landing.

"So, tell me about your time in Austin, then?" asked Jake.

Christina began, " People hear the word Texas and they visualise a longhorn skull bleached by the sun, cactus and miles of sand; maybe some oil wells with those nodding donkeys. In Austin, that could not be further from the truth. They say in Austin that its only problem is that it's surrounded by Texas."

"Austin is famed for its nightlife and is regularly dubbed "the drunkest city in the US". Austin is to Texas as Berlin is to Germany, which is to say it proudly, provocatively, perversely bears little resemblance to the rest of the state.

"Even its airport has kitted-out six performance stages where bands – hip hop, indie country, rock – play through arrivals and departures alike.

"Austinites are everything the rest of Texas despises; politically liberal, socially diverse, obsessed with the latest artful food fads, kooky vintage fashion, upcycled jewellery, nude swimming, community values and shopping local.

"Aha, like parts of London then, not so far from our office!" said Jake, " Except the swimming. Too cold."

Christina continued, " Pretty awesome, huh? You will need to say it while there -'Awesome!'

"I think I can do Awesome, " said Jake, " I've been doing UK lifestyle magazines for years."

"And Austin still does that elaborate Southern politeness that means even the simplest request – for a menu or directions or a hotel bill – must be book ended with a sincere "How are you today?" at the start and a heartfelt

"Have a nice day" to finish, " she continued, " It's the norm across the Deep South, but in Austin it just amps the sense that everybody is on holiday."

Christina smiled, " Jake, you'll have to imagine you are being a willing extra in one of those annoying, aspirational phone TV ads."

"You know the sort; achingly cool shiny happy people drinking craft beer and browsing antique stalls, complete with a scratchy fretted soundtrack of an earnest girl on an acoustic guitar singing about sunshine, swimming in the lake and everyday happiness."

"Right on, " said Jake, " I can do that." He reached into his seat pocked and produced his William Painter sunglasses, which he slid on his nose and hooked over his ears.

"That, in a nutshell, is Austin, " Jake could see Christina was smiling at the thought.

"So how did you come to be in Austin in the first place?" asked Jake.

"It's all about the music - as they say - I've always played musical instruments since I was tiny, my feet couldn't reach the pedals on our old upright pianos. It means that I have an instinct about what to play most of the time. It fits right in with the Austin vibe, " answered Christina,

"For example, when I was young, I could usually pick out the tunes from the TV adverts and replay them. We had a small farm, and my mother used to encourage my playing and she was really quite subtle about it."

Christina looked like she was remembering a distant

past, " When I was really young, we formed a band and used to play in the room with the piano. Other local kids came around and it was one of them that when much older - gave me a break to get into music."

"It meant that when I started taking the music seriously, I could play, sing, learn new tunes quickly and I was also used to playing with other folk. You know - letting them have their piece of the tune and being able to copy their playing style."

"So when I was touring with my first CD's worth of tunes, I could show up in somewhere like Austin and adapt to the musical climate."

"I was really excited to be in Austin the first time. There were so many accomplished musicians there, and I could tell that they were also instinctive rather than manufactured. Even someone like Stefani Germanotta (that's Lady Gaga) was able to both be glitzy and yet sizzle out a country and western vibe version of her electropop Born this Way.

Stefani and I were staying at the same hotel and I met her quietly sitting in the bar with one of the Pussycat Dolls - Kimberly Wyatt. They called me over and said they had recognised me from a poster - they knew how tough it was to get started in the business, which is what Clare had also told me.

"It turns out that Stefani had also been made to practice piano from an early age - in the Upper West Side - then she went to Creative Arts Camp, so we had some similarities, although she seemed to have about 50 creative projects on the go at any time.

I could hardly tell her about my side assignments with the Russian FSB or the *Glavnoye razvedyvatel'noye upravleniye* - you know, the GRU."

"You never fail to surprise, Christina, "

"The next time I was here, it was with Clare; I'd got some gigs around Austin for SWSX and Clare was handling the PR side of things. We'd arrived with a couple of boxes of CDs too and would give some away and sell others at the gigs."

"That was the time we stayed at a Marriott, which was opposite a Mexican Café and Cantina. They had a kind of Margarita machine there and Clare and I went along to find out how it worked."

Jake pulled a face, "Margarita machine sounds dangerous?"

Christina continued, " We were chatting away and I became conscious that both of us were earnestly putting the world to rights. You know that feeling when the room seems to shrink away from you? It comes a while after that little 'crack!' inside your skull. The one that reminds you to stop - like your brain saying, 'No.'

"It was too easy to point to the machine and get served two more slushy Margaritas. They tasted divine, but *Vá* did they provide a headache the next day. Clare, the ever professional, had put us off going to that bar until after all of my performances."

Christina paused for a moment, and then continued, " I can remember the next morning going out for a walk to clear our heads. Stetsons, tied-high check shirts, jeans, cowboy boots, shades. We were living a dream. We'd linked arms and were walking back along towards 6th street. It looked so different with everything closed and no-one around. The harsh sunlight showed the dust and reminded us that Austin has risen from the desert. It was still impressive how quickly the town had been reset overnight from the prior day's revelling.

"No, so I didn't get to see the corporate side, except I'd notice a few suited types in the crowds swirling around the night-time scene. I think there were several big corporations based in the area and I guess Sixth Street was the place to show visitors a good time."

An aircraft announcement cut into their conversation.

"Sounds like we are about to arrive, " said Jake.

Austin, Texas

They had booked into the Marriot and Christina had already looked outside for any signs of a Mexican restaurant with Margaritas.

"I think it is the same hotel, but I can't be sure." she said.

"It's late enough, " said Jake, " We need to be fresh for tomorrow. Let us recap our objectives."

"Okay, " said Christina,

"Interview them about the truck convoy. Photograph them and one of the trucks, Snoop around and steal things."

"Er, that last part - steal things? - You added that."

"Well only steal things if we think they are relevant, " said Christina, " And keep an eye open for anyone following us."

They both looked around. The entire lobby of the hotel was deserted.

"They are all out having fun on Sixth Street, " explained Christina.

Raven Headquarters

Christina and Jake were in the lobby of the hotel.

"08:30 for the pickup, " said Jake, " Clare arranged all of this."

"That's great, " said Christina, " Although, did you say that Raven were picking us up?"

"Yes, " said Jake, " Be careful then, said Christina, " As an agent I'd usually get my own car to their place."

"Why so?" asked Jake.

"A couple of reasons; first they can't listen in on our conversations and second they wouldn't know where we are staying. Its Espionage 101, " smiled Christina.

"Christina Nott, femme fatale, " whispered Jake.

"It's Hyde, " said Christina, " Remember?"

"Oops, " said Jake, " I'd make a rubbish spy."

A black Lincoln town car was pulling into the hotel entrance.

"I think this will be us, " said Christina, wheeling her Pelican Protector towards the door of the hotel.

"That's a lot of kit, " said Jake.

"Need to look the part, " said Christina.

"Spectator?" asked the driver, " That's right, " said Jake, thinking that he was not from the Spectator and this was an entirely freelance operation. Clare must surely have got it wrong in her PR explanation.

"It's about 20 minutes, " said the driver, " The building and campus is over by Walnut Creek. Assuming the MoPac is clear, that is, "

They climbed into the back of the coolly air-conditioned car. Even the short walk from the lobby to the vehicle had reminded them of how warm it could get in Texas.

And then they were on their way.

"Great view of the Capitol, " said Jake, looking out of the window, " We're heading straight for it, "

As if he'd heard, the driver took a left and then headed towards the Expressway. They were soon on a fast road, cutting through a flat area punctuated with corporate glass buildings.

Then an exit and a few minutes driving through fields,

interspersed with more plate glass and a few convenience stores.

Then a private driveway. They had arrived at Raven, a tall blue building, in a campus with several other smaller buildings. The site looked immense.

"We are going to Building 903, " said the driver. I'll drop you there and then there will be someone to meet you."

Jake looked at his original email from Clare.

They checked into the reception. Both Jake and Christina had photographs taken and were issued with passes.

"Can we get lanyards? Please?" asked Christina.

"Oh, why yes, of course, ma'am." The guard pulled a couple of light blue lanyards from his supply behind the desk.

"They have a little clip, here, let me show you. And someone will be here to collect you momentarily, you have a nice day now."

A few minutes later someone appeared, " Hello I'm Scott Eastin. You must be Ms Hyde and Mr Lambers, Welcome to Raven Headquarters. I am here to collect you and to show you to our Corporate Briefing Centre. There you will meet Mark McKown and Mary Spalding. It is only a short walk; you'll both be okay to follow me - or does anyone require special assistance?"

"That's fine, thank you, " said Jake, " We'll follow."

Scott walked them through some double doors and across a fairly plush looking break-out areas, then through a second set of double doors and they found themselves with an extensive view out across the gardens of Raven and a couple of water fountains and a small lake.

"Wow, you know how to make an impact, " said Jake, " This is very idyllic, "

"I guess we all get to take it for granted when we work here so much, " answered Scott.

"Say, I know we started early, if you had to skip breakfast, we've some prepared around the corner there."

He showed them to a buffet area, like any in a hotel, and Jake noticed that the food was anything from a large steak, through Texas style scrambled eggs, omelettes, tomatoes, bacon and a pile of waffles.

"Bigsy would like it here, " said Christina and Jake nodded.

" I guess some coffee would be great and maybe one of those bagels, " said Christina, " Me too, I think, " said Jake.

They grabbed a couple of the plates, the informal mugs and scooped up a modest breakfast each.

"Ah, I'm glad to see you've made yourselves at home, " said a voice, " Hello, I'm Mark McKown - welcome to the Corporate Briefing Centre."

"You must be Jake, and Christina, why hello."

And at that moment their second host appeared, along with another man. "Hello, you are all doing the introductions already! I'm Mary Spalding and this is Kevin Dubner."

They all shook hands and introduced themselves.

"Kevin was involved directly in that ambush in Iraq, I think he will be able to tell you about it. Look, I can see you have managed to grab some fixin's from our chef. We'll give Kevin a chance to grab a plate o' that steak and then we'll be off to one of the meeting rooms."

Christina and Jake realised that they were in a well-rehearsed process in the Corporate briefing centre. They would need to listen carefully for nuance in the words that were about to be spoken.

"We pride ourselves on our plain and simple southern hospitality here, " said Mark, " and it usually makes the chit chat move along real fine."

Jake was trying to work out whether the Southern-ness of the speech was being specially applied for his and Christina's benefit.

"Let's go over yonder to the meeting rooms, " said Mark.

The room was small, with a table and eight chairs, and seemed darker after the huge plate glass looking to the sunlight in the entrance area. It included a screen for presenting pictures and what looked like video recording facilities.

"Will the recording be on?" asked Christina, " We need to know for any copyright reasons."

"Oh, don't worry about that, " said Mary, " It's purely for archival purposes."

"Now let me tell you, we were madder than a wet hen about the original coverage of the ambush, " said Mark, " It implied that the US Army didn't help us. Even with the video footage."

"Let's hear it from Kevin, " said Jake, " After all he was there - and we've read that report quite thoroughly."

Kevin began, " Yes, it is like it shows in the report. We did get lost. A few of us were checking on our phones and had even told the convoy leader he'd taken a wrong turning.

"They said that it could have been our own phone chatter that alerted the insurgents."

"Then the first vehicle ran over the first IED. It took the track off the vehicle which rendered it static. It was when the guys tried to clamber out that the gunfire broke out."

"It sounded like machine gun fire, and we could see a red Toyota flatbed with a machine gun on the back. It looked like an NSTV Toyota Tacoma, with a belt-fed machine gun, such as a M240 or M249, fitted to a roll bar behind the cabin. It even looked as if the gun had a Raptor night sight fitted to it. And I could see the aerials and brackets for what looked like C4ISR - sorry I mean Command, Control, Communications, Computers, Intelligence, Surveillance and Reconnaissance mounts and wiring.

"Kevin, Could I stop you there for a moment?" asked Jake, " Your description is very precise. Have you been in the US Army, by any chance."

"Yes sir, I did my tour in Iraq. I guess the military training doesn't wear off."

"Sorry, can I ask a question too?" Interrupted Christina, " I notice you said NSTV - what does that mean?"

"Oh, Non-Standard Tactical Vehicle, ma'am - We use that term for modified commercial vehicles that could be used on special operations. The Tacomas were a standard USSOCOM configuration. A high-end one with raptor sights and C4ISR would be something of an exotic animal, but I am certain that was what we saw.

"It's also on the video that Victor took. It's the red 4-door pickup coated in sand, with what looks like a pile of junk in the back. I thought it also sounded petrol driven, which makes me think it was from Afghanistan. The Afghanistan ones had petrol instead of diesel engines because they were quieter."

"And what were you driving?"

"Well, I was a passenger, but we were in M939 trucks. You know, the standard US Army transport of choice in the desert. Our convoy was a mix of short and long wheelbase vehicles, and although they looked like army trucks, they all carried civilian markings too. They did not carry guns though. It is against the RoE to carry weapons on civilian trucks."

"The AFSOC - sorry Air Force Special Operations Command that was with us had made sure that the HUMVEES were tooled up. They were all up-armoured and carried enhanced weapons.

"You see a Hummer H4 in a commercial car park at the shopping mall and think of them as heavy duty. In the Army, we think of Hummers as light four-wheel drives, at least until they've been up-armoured. So much were they thought of as light that they've been mainly superseded by the JLTV now - oh that's the Joint Light Tactical Vehicle.

"You can see from this situation that a single Toyota with a rapid-fire machine gun doing death blossom could successfully ambush 12 trucks, and 5 Humvees.

"Death blossom?" asked Jake,

"Oh yeah, the tendency of Iraqi forces, in response to receiving a little fire from the enemy, to do the "death blossom" spraying fire indiscriminately in all directions. I think it comes from a Star Wars movie in which a single starfighter can single-handedly wipe out an entire armada, " answered Kevin.

"All, I think that Kevin has given more than enough information for your article, " interrupted Mark, " I think that, together with something from the original press release and some photographs should give you ample coverage."

Mary nodded, " Yes thank you Kevin, you have been most helpful."

"We'll take some photographs now, " said Christina, " I suggest a couple indoors here, portrait style, and then a couple outside with the truck."

Christina unpacked some equipment from the large case and set it up. "I'll take a couple of quick test shots to get the lighting right, " she said, " and then a couple more of you, Kevin."

Jake said, " We are not sure of a format yet- so we'll probably want pictures to cover every eventuality - that's both portrait and landscape format so our editors have options when they lay it out in the publication."

Christina worked away on some photographs for several minutes. Then she announced, " That's good, I'm done. Can we go outside now?"

"Sure, " said Mark, " I think Mary will accompany this part of the visit. We don't want you getting lost in here, do we?"

"Yes, and maybe a couple of office shots on the way to the truck?" said Christina.

"I'll see what we can do, " said Mary.

They all walked back to the main entrance. Mark said his goodbyes and wished them all a mighty fine day. Mary accompanied them to the swing door area.

"We've, a utility vehicle coming to collect us for the short ride to the transportation depot, " she said, " Christina, I hope that won't be too difficult for you with that case?"

"Not at all, " said Christina, " I'm used to it."

They clambered aboard the minibus that arrived, and the driver told them it would be around a five-minute ride to the transportation depot.

Jake noticed that they were weaving their way around the Raven campus and, after a few minutes arrived at a fenced-off compound.

Compound

They climbed from the bus, and Kevin said, " They said they have prepared the vehicle for us, I guess that means they have cleaned it."

"It is not one of the actual trucks used in Iraq, but it is the same type, " said Kevin, " Look, I don't think you'll want to get that Texas tag in any of the photographs."

"Thanks Kevin and well spotted, " said Christina.

"I'd like a couple of moody shots from alongside the cab, I think we can hide the tag if we do that, " Christina made ready a reflector and the camera, " See I'm using the reflector like we do with models, to bring out the detail!" smiled Christina.

"So, I'm a model now!" laughed Kevin, " Don't tell the guys!"

"That was excellent, " said Christina, " I think you've nailed it, look here's my card." She passed a Bluefish card to Kevin.

"Bluefish?" He queried, " Yes, I'm on hire to the magazine for this story, " said Christina.

"Oh, I get it - like a lot of us contractors, " said Kevin.

"That's fine, " interrupted Mary, " I think you've enough for the story now. I'll call the Town Car to take you back to your hotel. And thank y'all for visiting Raven like this. It is a long way to come for the story, "

"Yes, but we want to get it right, " said Jake, " And thank you, Mary and Kevin, for being so helpful."

On cue, the Lincoln Town Car appeared inside the compound. Jake and Christina said their farewells and were on their way.

What did we learn?

Christina and Jake kept quiet on the journey back to central Austin. They arrived in the Marriot and Christina said to Jake, " Twenty minutes, back here? Then we can talk."

Twenty minutes later they met again. Christina had moved the big case into her room. They had both showered and changed from the clothes they had worn around the transportation compound.

"First thing we need to do is change hotels, " said Christina, " There's a Four Seasons across the way. I just don't feel happy that Raven know where we are staying. I want us to do the re-booking, not leave it to this hotel."

"Sounds like a plan, said Jake, " if somewhat paranoid."

"Only the paranoid survive" said Christina, quoting Andy Grove, the ex-CEO of Intel. "See, we learned some things from the west when we were going through training!"

"We seemed to pick up several things, I'm not sure that Kevin was supposed to say some of them, " said Jake.

Christina agreed, " The biggest was the Toyota truck tricked out like a US Special Ops vehicle. That whole scenario seemed highly dubious."

"I thought that Kevin was highly dubious, too, " said Jake, " Like someone trying too hard. All that detail about Non-Standard Tactical Vehicles - The Tacoma as a USSOCOM configuration with raptor sights and C4ISR. Nothing like planting the evidence."

Christina continued, "I'll buy the stuff about M939s being used in the convoy. Although that truck, they showed us for the photo wasn't a 939 or anywhere near to it.

"Trust me, that's an M977 eight-wheel drive, 10-ton diesel truck. A HEMTT in battle-field jargon. Heavy Expanded Mobility Tactical Truck (HEMTT).

"I'm no specialist on this stuff, but anyone would know the difference, especially if you've been in a front-line operation position. You really want to know how well protected you'll be when you take a ride, " Christina thought back to the times she was bounced about around the fields of Bulgaria in miscellaneous trucks while she studied at the Vasil Levsky National Military University.

Christina added, " I'm amazed that Kevin didn't say anything, whilst he stood next to a truck which usually carries containers. It makes me not quite trust the rest of his pitch to us, like we should take it all in because we are hearing it from a veteran who has been in harm's way.

Jake said, " Yes but the other thing about that truck was the civilian markings. Yes, it had Texan number plates, but did you see where it had the civilian designations. It also had company of origin markings. It didn't say Raven, nor Qube. No, it said Brant."

"Yes, I even managed to get a photo of that, " said Christina.

"So, are we moving out, or what?" said Jake.

Touchdown

There was a screech as the wheels touched down.

"Back in Heathrow, and we didn't even get to Sixth Street," said Christina.

"It'll do my reputation no-good with Clare, " said Jake.

"Too much at stake, " said Christina, " We needed to quietly disappear that evening."

Christina called Antanov, to check whether he could meet her at the Triangle offices. Jake similarly called Chuck. This would be an interesting mission debrief.

They took the Heathrow Express back to Paddington and then hopped onto the tube around to Liverpool Street. They decided it was simpler to cab the last part to save dragging the large camera case along the street.

They arrived in the offices to see everyone present; Jake,

Bigsy, Chuck, Antanov and Clare. Clare asked, " Did you get my message?"

They looked at each other. They had switched their phones back on at Heathrow but been in Tube tunnels from Paddington until the cab ride right at the end.

"Sorry Clare, no we haven't" said Jake, " What is it?"

"It's all off, Raven have asked us to pull the story, No explanation, just an apology."

"Interesting, " said Christina, " Wait until you hear the story anyway, "

"Well, as we were never intending to publish it, I think we can call it a result!" said Jake.

"I seem to remember once before you had a story pulled - about Darren Collins actually, and that got us into a lot of hot water, " said Bigsy.

"Okay, well this one will take some beating, " said Jake.

"We are not even sure if the person we met as a civilian from the Iraq confrontation is really genuine, " said Christina.

"Here's how it played out. They were nice as pie to us, gave us access to Kevin Dubner from the Iraq mission. He told us about the ambush. His story was generally consistent with the news report"

"Except for one thing, " said Jake, " The Iraqi intercept of the convoy. It seemed to have been done in a Special Ops Toyota, kitted out with all the latest tech."

"It makes no sense, " said Clare, " Why would America Special Ops attack an American convoy?"

"Well, Kevin gave us other information too. Chapter and verse of detail - too much detail in some cases. Remember those Russians with the Novichok at Salisbury? It was a bit like that, reciting Cathedral detail that could have come from a script."

"Then we went to take some photos outside in the vehicle compound. He'd given us all of that detail but was then quite happy to stand next to an entirely wrong kind of truck for the photographs."

"We decided that Raven were putting up a story and then deflecting us to the wrong trail. If we had published something, it would have been a new definitive account, which was good for them, but with a few accidental errors embedded in it which could have destroyed credibility. I think that is why they pulled it."

"Oh yes, and the last thing, the truck that we photographed. In its desert camo colours. It was a civilian badged truck from…Brant."

Primal Barrier

Pearly gates look more like a picket fence
Once you get inside 'em
Got friends but can't invite them

All the good girls go to hell
'Cause even God herself has enemies
And once the water starts to rise
And Heaven's out of sight
She'll want the Devil on her team

Billie Eilish

Antanov Analysis

"To a Russian mind this is altogether more straightforward, " said Antanov, " Let's consider."

"Correct, " said Christina, " To begin with, remember what Antanov explained a few days ago about oil conflicts."

"Oh yes, " said Clare, " The eight mechanisms, "

"We only need to throw one or two into the mix, " said Antanov, " oil-related grievances, whereby the presence of foreign workers in petrostates helps extremist groups such as al-Qaida recruit locals; and oil-related obstacles to multilateral cooperation, such as when an importer's attempt to curry favour with a petrostate prevents multilateral cooperation on security issues."

"So, think about it, " said Christina, " We've got America attempting to salvage the Iraqi situation and then insurgents running interference across it. Bingo. America will need to stay in Iraq and even shore up its presence against the petro-aggressors."

"I make that 2, 7 and 8 from my original list, all by sending in one Toyota Tacoma with a machine gun on the back. Admittedly it's a US Special Ops Toyota, but no-one needs to know, " said Antanov.

"Chuck, do you have any thoughts?" asked Christina.

"Em, not really, it is entirely plausible. To be honest it's the sort of thing I've been asked to do in the past, " said Chuck, "Although I'll always deny it."

Christina added, "Then we can add in the loyal flavour of Raven's subsidiaries supporting all of the Iraqi infrastructure reconstruction. It casts Raven as 'good guys' suffering in a conflict zone."

"You've thought this through, " said Jake, " While I was watching another Marvel movie on the plane."

"Not really, " said Christina, " Antanov and I are just distilling some of the thinking from our training. Maybe it was old KGB manuals, but some of the manoeuvres still seem to work."

Warp-speed farewell

They were back at Christina's flat.

"Christina, it's been good, " said Antanov.

Christina looked towards him, " It really has."

"This is the 'I'm going now' speech?" asked Christina.

"Yes, that'd be the one, " said Antonov, " I don't know what to say - except 'Thank you'!"

"You've been more than hospitable, " said Antanov, " But I can see you still live at warp-speed. You've been to Germany and to Austin while I've been staying here, as well as to the fancy Masonic event - For me - just the Masonic event is already a highlight."

"I know, " said Christina, " I feel privileged to have had so many lives too. Like a cat. Iceland, Russia, Bulgaria, New York, Vancouver, London, Milan, Paris, Amsterdam and back here again."

"You are already past nine lives, " said Antanov,

"And past nine loves, " said Christina adding, " If you

only count the men, "

They both laughed, in a higher pitched voice Christina added, " But I'm working on the score for women."

Antanov said, " Look, shall I move out tomorrow? When you are at the office? If you need anything more on the Masons, you now know how to contact me."

Christina nodded and closed to embrace Antanov.

"Remember I positioned you into that last shindig as a Rosicrucian adept. You had that discreet rose with the cross, but it pushes you towards the Golden Dawn of theurgic spiritual development. Put another way, it's heavy shit. Consider it a woman's shortcut to the top of the pyramid."

Christina looked thoughtful, " Strangely enough, I met a fortune teller named Roberta the day before I made contact with you. He said that I should steer clear of the crystal balls, although he deduced, I had exceptional scrying powers. I'd never heard of scrying - it's like divination through staring into objects, but it does tie in with some of my Icelandic gods."

"You are moving outside of the Rosicrucian thought now; it will blow the minds of rank-and-file Freemasons."

"Yes, but as an edge creature one gets to notice the low-level fluctuations in the stability of edges, " said Christina.

"You have passed beyond me and there is little I can add, Oh Archangel, my dearest " said Antanov smiling, " Let me kiss you and then I will be gone."

Accessories

Bernard had been intrigued to receive the invitation from Sir Charles Frobisher. A private dinner and a chance to meet with a couple of Formula One racing heroes. Sir Charles had hinted that Bernard Driscoll might even be on the same table as one of them and to wait to hear from an enchanting A-lister who would be his +1 for the evening.

Now was the day of the dinner and Bernard was still reeling from being contacted by Marion Charlotte who she informed was to be his +1.

He'd had to google Marion to make sure. He remembered that this stunning A-lister looked a lot like Audrey Tautou in her Priceless era. She would certainly turn heads at the dinner, and he knew she was rumoured to have had assignations with various Formula One drivers.

Sir Charles had been careful to point out that this was a very private function and that there would not be any press present. Indeed, he described it as a quiet meeting of the Brotherhood, with some delightful accessories.

Bernard wasn't sure about this last part. It seemed to him

that the event was skating close to the President's Club in terms of its presentation style.

He remembered that the 360 guests at the President's Club annual dinners – all men – included leading figures in business, entertainment and politics. They would pay for a dinner and participate in auctions of such prizes as meetings with influential people. The proceeds would go to charities, including children's charities, and other organisations.

It all sounded innocuous enough, but then the *Financial Times* sent two undercover reporters to join the 130 scantily clad "hostesses" specially hired for the event by the Artista agency. It reported that several of the guests had harassed or assaulted the hostesses in the course of the evening.

Bernard was sure he did not want to get into anything like that, although the thought of attending this event with an A-lister on his arm was too good to let pass.

The dinner was set to be held at The Dorchester, which Bernard viewed warily as an echo from the President's Club days.

Marion had suggested they meet in China Tang before the main event. It was a cocktail bar conveniently attached to the hotel and Bernard was happy to follow this plan.

Marion was stunning and Bernard could feel the endorphins of pleasure sweeping through his body as he approached her.

"Bernard! So glad you are accompanying me this

evening, you will be able to tell me all about how things work in Parliament!"

"Only if you'll tell me about some of your racing driver friends!" he replied.

"That's a little saucy, for an opening line, " twinkled Marion, " First, let's have a cocktail, maybe trade a little gossip and then we can go through to the main event."

Soon, she took his arm and they climbed the stairs out of the bar in Tang's and walked around to the main hotel entrance.

"You are here for the special event?" enquired the doorman, " You'll need to follow my colleague over there."

He pointed towards a very primly turned out female host.

"This way please, oh. and could you have your invitations ready? There are a few formalities on the way in, for security reasons."

They arrived at the understated security area. There was an electronic arch, artfully decked out in flowers. They walked through in single file and on the other side Marion was given a tiny bouquet of exquisite miniature flowers.

"Something pretty for your table, " said the security person.

Marion took the flowers and the two of them walked towards the main doors. They entered a ballroom which had been laid out with many large circular tables. At the front entrance was a plan which showed where they would sit.

Bernard read off the list of names. He was to sit on a table with two racing legends. A current Formula One driver for Ferrari, and a British racing legend from the Hall of Fame.

Next to him, he noticed, was his contact from ISMC, Gerhardt Schmidt. He wondered if Schmidt would be bringing Nina, his blonde partner as well. The listing unchivalrously just said +1. He noticed that his partner Marion Charlotte was spelled out in full.

He could feel Marion moving on his arm. It gave him chills. She whispered in his ear, " I think we have a good table, and look, there's that film actress, the one in that movie sweeping all the awards. I think she is on the next table. " More chills.

Bernard thought all of his cards had come up at once as he sat at his place around the table.

"Hi Bernard, " said a familiar voice, it was Gerhardt. He squeezed Bernard on the shoulder and said, " This is quite an occasion! That's twice recently that I've seen you at something in London. Have you met my partner? Here's the lovely Marina, and Hello, you must be Marion Charlotte. I have heard so much about you!"

Bernard said his greetings to Marina and mentally noted that she had similar length blonde hair to Nina, who he had met at the last event.

At that moment a small choir struck up. They were singing something mournful and pretty. Bernard did not recognise it.

"It's Leonard Cohen, " said Marion, " 'Anthem', I think, I believe it is about political and social justice- beautiful, how they are singing it, " she gestured towards the singers.

"Well Hello EEEEEveryyyyy-one," blasted out a compere. Bernard was vaguely aware that this man on the television. Irish, he thought, possibly gay. He was giving it some this evening.

They listened to the introductions, which then passed over to Sir Charles Frobisher who gave a short earnest speech and mentioned that there would be an inspirational rock-climber and a rock band during the rest of the evening.

"Thank God it is not someone from X-Factor, " murmured Marion, " At least they've got someone who has earned their way here."

Bernard wasn't very up to date with his musical choices. He'd liked the Beatles, and his hall-mates had played some of those progressive bands like The Genesis and The Pink Floyd. The music scene to him nowadays was a mystery.

They were well into their main course before Gerhardt cut into the conversation again.

"I hope you are enjoying the evening; Sir Charles would probably appreciate it if you said a small thank you to him in private. I believe he is seeing people in a small suite. You won't need to worry about Marion though, she will realise what you are doing, and I'll keep her amused whilst you are away."

Bernard stiffened. This didn't sound like a suggestion. More like an order, and it was one that he realised he'd better follow up.

He whispered to Marion, " I'll be going to see Sir Charles soon, to say thank you."

"Yes dear, you probably should, " she whispered back in his ear. Driscoll could feel the autonomous sensory meridian response as a tingling sensation in his scalp and down the back of the neck, in response to her gentle whisper. What was in that main course? Or was it purely his response to Marion?

He stood to find the room with Sir Charles Frobisher. No sooner had he done so than one of the attentive waiting staff guided him to one side, checked what he wanted and then escorted him to Frobisher's room.

Cohiba

"Come in, dear boy, come in, " Said Sir Charles affably, to Bernard Driscoll.

"This room somehow reminds me of The Peck, " said Sir Charles, making a reference to one of the quadrangles of Christ Church at Oxford University.

In a phrase, Sir Charles had distanced himself from the red-bricked Driscoll.

"Come sit down here, have a cigar, " said Frobisher, pulling Driscoll further into the web.

"Can we smoke in here?" asked Bernard,

"Well, I can't think why they'd keep a humidor in here, unless we can jolly well use it, " said Frobisher.

"Here, have a Cohiba, " he gestured towards the cabinet. They each selected a cigar.

Frobisher cut the end from his and offered to Driscoll, " Shall I?"

"Thank you, " Then Frobisher produced a butane lighter,

"We could light them from the cedar wood spills, but I think this way is just as effective and doesn't mar the taste."

They were both lit up.

"I want to thank you, for tonight's experience, " said Driscoll, " It is really something rather special, "

"Not at all, my good man, "said Sir Charles, " It must make a break for you being so highly bound up in all of that state work."

"It is, and the delightful company too."

"Oh, has Gerhardt been up to something I don't know about?" asked Sir Charles.

"My Plus One for the evening is Marion Charlotte, " replied Driscoll.

"How divine, " said Sir Charles, " Although, I should warn you, coming to see me like this, she will probably have flown away. You'll need to cherish what little time you did spend with her."

Bernard suddenly chilled. He was having an ASMR flashback to her whispering in his ear.

"Of course, that needn't be the end of it, "said Sir Charles.

"You seem to be well-established now as a member of the Brotherhood, " he continued.

"Em, I'm not supposed to be involved with those kinds of organisations, " replied Driscoll.

"No, and neither should you be," answered Sir Charles, "That's why we try so hard to protect the members. No point in being a secret organisation if we can't have secrets!"

"But I can remember not so many years ago when Theresa May came down heavy on Freemasons and similar organisations."

"Ah yes, Theresa May went to the Police Federation conference and ripped into it. The Federation had to decide whether it would adopt a package of 36 reforms, with May, who was then home secretary, threatening that if it failed to do so, it would be taken over by the government and forced to. Ironically, her government got overruled by Parliament, so that was the end of it."

Sir Charles continued, " Of course, Parliament has its own lodges too, one for ex-MPs and another for the Press lobby.

Sir Charles looked towards Driscoll, " You'll have heard of New Welcome Lodge, which was set up to recruit MPs, peers and parliamentary staff?"

He continued, " There's also Gallery Lodge, established for members of the political press corps known as the lobby.

"Both remain active, although the United Grand Lodge of England says that no MPs or lobby journalists are members of those lodges.

"And it doesn't stop MPs from being Freemasons.

He paused to take a puff of cigar.

"These Cubans know how to make a fine cigar, " he said.

"So, let me tell you about something that I think you'll find interesting and let me introduce you to someone else."

He plucked a slim phone from his pocket, " James, can you drop in on us now, please?"

He pushed the phone back in his pocket.

"Captain James Wylie is a bit of a specialist on matters related to Iraq. He was out there serving Queen and Country, including time in Basra, before we handed everything back to the Iraqis."

"That was almost like a siege?" queried Driscoll.

"Oh, it was a siege, all right, " said a voice, James strode into the room, shook both their hands and sat down on a chair facing Driscoll and Frobisher.

"Hello Charles, Hello Mr Driscoll, I'm James Wylie. Charles invited me to paint the picture for you.

Frobisher offered him a cigar, which he declined. "I gave up smoking in Iraq. Too much hassle. There were never enough smokes around. The US soldiers used to get theirs at TCPs - that's Traffic Control Points. They'd see an Iraqi car with smokers in it, flag it down and then ask for a cigarette. The Iraqis - not wanting trouble - used to give a whole pack - sometimes a carton. It made those checkpoints unreliable.

James continued, " They were supposed to be looking for

car bombs, not packets of Marlboro. Then there was the red cherry of a lit cigarette at night, which would compromise your position. Snipers, spotters, you know."

Driscoll could sense that this man must have had PTSD after his return. It seemed that dragging up memories was going to pay its price.

James continued, " The Basra airport base was constantly hit, upwards of dozens of times a day, by mortar and rocket fire. Yet, despite the weight of fire, there was relatively little disruption to operations, as considerable effort had been put into Force Protection measures.

"These included passive measures on the base, such as physical hardening of structures, and active measures, such as fighting patrols conducted by RAF Regiment squadrons in the Base's ground defence area, beyond the perimeter.

"We used external contractors to bolster parts of the infrastructure. For the passive measures, that sort of thing.

"We could better do our job of aggressive patrolling activity. It denied the militias the opportunity to use the airport's ground defence area for launching anything other than a small number of rockets.

Driscoll asked, " Didn't that just push back their aggressive position?"

"It did. It forced the militias to use firing points that were further away, which meant that larger rockets, with correspondingly larger warheads were used.

"More than 300 rockets hit the airport in the two months

between June and August. Sniper attacks were also a deadly and common occurrence for British service personnel as well as IED attacks on patrols that were going out of the bases.

"At times, even when it was blazingly hot, we'd walk around the camp in full battle rattle to avoid snipers and other kinds of attacks."

James paused as if thinking.

"The IED attacks and organised ambushes also hit convoys from the airport that were transporting food, fuel, ammunition and other equipment. Convoys were primarily used for this task because helicopters were at high risk from being shot down.

Bernard asked, " I know that that was traumatic, but it was still quite a few years ago, wasn't it?"

Charles nodded, " Yes, but even now, the Americans are still hesitant about how to handle Iraq. For example, even in 2020, there was that MQ-9 Reaper drone of the U.S. Air Force which launched several missiles targeting General Soleimani, striking his convoy as it departed the airport, engulfing two cars in flames and killing 10 people. That was ordered by Trump."

Sir Charles cut in, " Some could say it was a President posturing for acceptance. The US President asserted that Soleimani had been planning further attacks on American diplomats and military personnel and had approved the attack on the American embassy in Baghdad.

"According to Saudi-based Arab News, the drone that

struck Soleimani's convoy had been launched from Al Udeid Air Base in Qatar.

James picked up, " Yes, a statement by the Air Force of Iran's Islamic Revolution Guards Corps stated that Ali Al Salem Air Base in Kuwait participated, among other bases in the region, in the operation that was executed near Baghdad airport.

James continued, " Then Kuwait summoned the Iranian ambassador to Kuwait over the statement and expressed Kuwait's resentment and categorical denial at such statement.

Sir Charles added, " These skirmishes led to something of an impasse. It wasn't repositioned by the Press, but the day after the strike, the US had to send in the 1st Airborne Brigade Combat Team, 82nd Airborne Division, deployed to the Middle East. So more boots on the ground and more infrastructure support required."

James continued, " Yes, and so it went on, Iraqi state news reported that the day after the drone strike there had been another airstrike against a convoy of medical units of the Iraqi Popular Mobilisation Forces near Camp Taji in Taji, north of Baghdad."

Sir Charles added, " But we were into Fake News by this time. An Iraqi Army source told Reuters the attack killed six people and critically wounded three. The PMF later said there was no senior commander in the convoy, and the Imam Ali Brigades denied reports of the death of its leader."

"The PMF also denied that any medical convoy was targeted at Taji. There was no information about who conducted the attack. A spokesperson for Operation Inherent Resolve said the coalition did not do it, while Iraq's Joint Operations Command denied reports of any such attack, saying it was a false rumour that spread quickly due to the prior airport strike."

James continued, " To be honest, it's impossible to know who to believe. We sometimes used to watch the Ali Baba television stations and they would show American planes flying along the perimeters blowing up comms or munitions. Then we'd check and no-one would know about the operation."

Sir Charles added, " We are getting more examples of these kinds of things. There is going to be increased pressure to corral the effects. It is extremely likely that the UK would be called in. That is unless it can head this off at the pass."

Sir Charles looked at Bernard Driscoll, " Think about it. The UK can either send politically sensitive troops into these areas, or they can head off the problem, paving the way for infrastructure reconstruction and secure stability through the judicious sale of munitions.

"A quiet influence behind the scene is all that is required to make this run along nicely. That's where we think you could be instrumental in stopping the violence and helping the trade position simultaneously.

James nodded, " There's got to be diplomatic ways to contain this."

Sir Charles continued, " Bernard, there's less overt glory in this path, but every opportunity to benefit greatly and without personal sacrifice. And to top it all, you'd be one of several people of influence to make this happen."

"I'll need to think about this, " said Bernard. After he had finished thinking about Marion's whisper in his ear from earlier.

The American Station

"It is still bugging me, " said Amanda.

"What is? " asked Chuck.

They were sitting on the balcony of Chuck's hotel in central London.

The skyline was on fire as the sun tiptoed towards the west. They had both ordered a cocktail - A Peachy Canchanchara and a Golden South Sea Pearldiver - from the bar downstairs that was several times named the best cocktail bar in the world. Just after it won the last prize, it mysteriously changed its name from Dandelyan to the Lyan-ess.

"...That the Americans would set up a listening station along the Thames. Almost exactly on my spot, " said Amanda, " ...And that you have such an outrageous expenses budget, "

"We should dig some more, " said Chuck, " But we'll need to be careful not to trip any wires. Let's make it a priority tomorrow."

...

Amanda was already on the phone when Chuck awoke. He waited patiently for her to finish.

She started, " I've called through to GCHQ. To Grace Fielding. We go back. Turns out that GCHQ know all about the listening station - more - laughably than the CIA."

"How can that be?" asked Chuck.

"I wondered that myself. It turns out that in the Land of the Free everything is fair game for outsourcing. That's what the CIA have done. They've outsourced the station."

"Incredible!" said Chuck, " But then, I suppose, come to think of it that's only what they do with people like me."

"Big difference. You go doing things that are Black Ops. They need the deniability. A listening station is, well, at the core of things."

"I bet it doesn't cost any less to run, either, " said Chuck, " You still need to hire the same number of people and to secure it."

"Well it seems that a friendly contractor has managed to convince the DoD and the CIA that they are capable. It's a company called Qube."

"I know Qube - they are part of Raven, aren't they?" asked Chuck.

"Very good, " said Amanda, " And according to Grace they do their job quite well. They are comparable to Blackstone Defense Services or some of the units that Halliburton runs."

"That's pretty broad spectrum, " said Chuck, " Everything from a so-called woman-owned small business to a mega-corporation."

"Well it goes to show who the US will do business with nowadays..." said Amanda, " And there's always pages of jobs advertised by both of them, in Counter Intelligence, right up to Top Secret."

"It's a little bit crazy, really, isn't it?" said Chuck, " Nothing like those old spy novels."

"I agree, " said Amanda, " But we've got to live with progress I suppose. Look, I need to get back into the office, there's a few other things on my plate right now. I could almost walk to Vauxhall Cross from here!"

"But you'll take a cab, I assume?" suggested Chuck, " I'm not going anywhere tonight, but tomorrow I'll need to check in with the Triangle gang."

Tap on the window

It was already past sunset. Clare and Bigsy were still in the Triangle offices. Clare was searching internet records and Bigsy was trying to piece together a trail from phone links.

An adjacent streetlight was shining in through the window at the back of the office and both Clare and Bigsy had their desk lights on. Bigsy had also rigged up some computer lights to come on around the edges of the office and to give some illusion of sunlight.

There was a commotion outside. A scraping sound. Then a tap on a window.

Clare looked up. It was too heavy to have been the yard cat that played around the area and occasionally spooked her by staring straight into the office.

A second tap and then a crash.

The window. It sounded as if something had hit it quite hard. Bigsy was running towards Clare. He tugged her by the hand.

"Come on Clare, we need to go into the back office, " as they ran, they heard a clunk as if something had dropped in from the window. Then a bang and a hissing sound.

"What the F...!" said Bigsy, " Stay back Clare, I don't think either of us need to be brave about this!" Another crash and suddenly they could hear the fire alarm.

"Don't open that door, " said Bigsy, " We'll have to go out through the back."

With that, he pulled at Clare's arm and then quietly slipped the lock on the back door to their offices. He opened it slowly, not wanting to make a sound.

"Quietly, " he said to Clare.

They slipped outside. Clare could hear her pulse banging in her head.

The back yard was silent and well-lit by a different streetlamp.

"We'll wait here for ten minutes, " said Bigsy, reaching for his phone from his pocket.

He dialled 999. After a quiet conversation with someone he spoke more loudly to Clare.

"I was calling the police, but the Emergency Services said they had already been alerted. Apparently, our building is on fire and the alarm has tripped to Jake.

"Fire engine is on its way. The police will turn up now I've requested them. I think we will be safe to go outside into the street.

"They gingerly opened the back gate and peered outside.

No people, but Bigsy could see smoke and a small orange glow from the broken window.

"It's on fire all right, " he said to Clare, " but whoever did it has made a run for it."

Clare looked like she was in shock to Bigsy.

"Here, let's sit down on the pavement and wait for the emergency services."

As he spoke, a fire tender appeared. It was flashing its blue lights but not making any sounds. It seemed to take up the whole street."

"It's there, " said Bigsy pointing, and then realised that the professional firefighter would know what a fire looked like. Clare laughed and Bigsy thought some good had come out of his stupid statement.

One of the firefighters came along to them, " Are you the owners?" he asked,

"Yes, we work here - we were working inside when it happened. Something through that window, " Bigsy pointed.

"Okay, was anyone else inside?"

"No just us, we got out through the back."

"Okay, we'll be here for a while and I'm afraid we might make some mess of your property. We will try to save whatever we can. Are there any canisters, paint cans or other types of flammables inside?"

"No, it's just a regular office, with papers and computers,

very normal, " said Clare.

"Okay, so my men won't come across anything unexpected inside then?" asked the firefighter.

Bigsy realised that the firefighter had a body camera and that he'd recorded everything. Bigsy remembered that he had put some small cameras around the outside of the office and that some of them might have recorded something from the event. He decided to stay quiet about this until he could take a look himself. He was glad that he had rigged the cameras to record to the Cloud instead of to a hard drive in the office.

Now it was the turn of the police. Another blue flashing light but no sound. Bigsy wondered why the need for stealth but he realised that there could be people around and they may not wish to disturb them. Certainly, he'd expected a small crowd to gather but so far there were only a couple of bystanders.

Clare, " You'd better take some footage of this, " said Bigsy, thinking that it might take Clare's mind off the shock.

Clare fiddled in her jeans and found her smartphone. "I'll take a few shots, but it is all quite upsetting, " she said.

A police officer was talking to the fireman and now made his way over to Bigsy.

"Here we go again, " thought Bigsy, as he prepared to answer the policeman's questions.

PART THREE

Secret Agent

Fire in the disco
Fire in the Taco Bell
Fire in the disco
Fire in the gates of hell

Electric Six - Danger! High Voltage

Diversion

Chuck's taxi approached the area of the Triangle Offices.

"Sorry Mate, There's some road diversion around here. They're always doing that. You don't know from one day to the next. Look, I can do a 'U' turn here, then we can cut up Shipton Street if you like and try to get into the area from the other end?"

"That's okay, " said Chuck, " You can drop me here"

"You know where you are? You'll have to go up past the roadblock and then take a left?"

"Yes, that's fine, " said Chuck, who after three visits thought he knew the area quite well.

"Card or cash, Mate?"

Chuck handed over a note, " It is okay, keep the change,"

"You sure mate? Thanks."

Chuck walked the hundred or so yards towards the Triangle offices. He could see Clare along the road.

"Chuck!" she said, " It is a bit of a mess. Our building caught fire yesterday evening. Bigsy and I were inside when it happened."

"No one hurt?" asked Chuck.

"No - we got out okay - thanks to Bigsy. Although Jake was called by the fire alarm company, by the time he arrived it was all over."

They stood outside of the building, which had been cordoned off with some blue and white tape.

"I see the police have been, " said Chuck., " They've cordoned it off, are they still here?"

"No, there was just a small fire car here. They said they were checking that the fire was fully out. They've gone now. Jake says he's called for the insurers to come take a look."

"Where's Jake then?"

"We decided to adjourn to the pub at the end of the street. He's in there with Bigsy and Christina."

"I think I'll take a quick look inside before we go join them, " said Chuck.

He ducked under the tape and walked gingerly towards the front entrance to the office. He could see the side window broken by what looked as if someone had tossed a brick through it.

He pushed against the front door which opened easily. The Fire Brigade must have smashed their way in. The main office area stank of burnt wood and everything was coated in damp soot. It didn't look as if even the metallic computers had survived the scale of the heat.

Chuck looked across to the window that had been broken. There was no sign of a brick or anything solid. There was an indentation in the floor. It looked to Chuck as if it was the source of the fire. The heat had been sufficient to crack the concrete and left a rough clinker-like edge. The whole area was blackened, and it looked as if there was molten metal in the dip in the concrete.

"Thermate, " said Chuck, to himself. He looks around, and the source of the fire was unmistakably where he was looking. He could see that the blackened area formed an approximate sphere around the area, as well as where furniture items had separately caught alight.

He noticed that the doors were still intact. Despite the obvious flames, the fire integrity of the office had prevented more than smoke from spreading. Chuck could not tell the type of doors, but he knew that the cheapest fire doors lasted 30 minutes and he'd expect an office door to last for an hour, on average.

He deduced from this that the fire had probably tipped the alarm and then been quite speedily dealt with by the Fire Brigade.

He stood up and walked back to Clare, who was still waiting outside.

"It's a mess, isn't it?" she said still in some shock at the events.

"Yes, " said Chuck, " Let's talk to the others."

They walked the short distance to the pub. It was a half-timbered kind of affair, and inside was more reminiscent of a locals' boozer than anything that out-of-towner would frequent.

Chuck was initially taken aback - then he heard Jake calling.

"Hey Chuck, Clare, we're here." They had grabbed a large table by a window. Chuck and Clare joined them as Bigsy stood to say, " What'll it be then?"

They ordered and Bigsy made his way to the bar.

"It's a mess, isn't it?" Said Jake, " Not an accident either, Bigsy and Clare heard the fire-setter. We were trying to work out why and who?"

Christina looked towards Chuck, " An M14-TH3 incendiary grenade was the fire starter. Look I even found a piece of the casing."

She showed Chuck a piece of charred Orange casing. It still showed the lettering M14/EN/H -in purple letters arranged underneath one another.

"Yes, I thought so too, Thermate as the incendiary - those grenades make their own oxygen. They even work under water."

"I remember them, " said Christina, " We used to practice some things with NATO ones when I was in Bulgaria."

The others looked around. Bulgaria, another part of Christina's past emerging.

"How would anyone get hold of one of these?" said Chuck, " I thought London was supposed to be pretty tight on such things."

"It is, " said Clare, " It would have to come from a defence contractor or an army base."

"Well, I know I'm stating the obvious, " said Chuck, " But it has to be because of your trip to the listening station."

"But how would they follow us?" said Bigsy.

"Something I've recently discovered, " said Chuck, " That listening station isn't a fully US Government run facility. It might have some CIA, but it is actually run by Qube, which is a subsidiary of Raven. Now Qube might have some extra facilities that the US wouldn't ordinarily use."

"Such as?" asked Bigsy.

"Well, think about it. You and Christina go to Qube. You ask a few innocuous questions, Bigsy steals a badge and a lanyard. If I was Qube after that then I'd want to check out anyone unusual in the building."

"You both turned up with your phones. It doesn't take a genius to see that they have probably logged your phones on the way in through reception. I know it is now illegal, but they have probably used the same tech that is being used to track viruses and virus contact points, ever since that global pandemic."

Chuck continued, " Piece it together. They've got your

photos, and your phone identities. All they need to do from their - wait for it - listening station - is to track your numbers. They can find where you live and where you work. I expect they were worried about the missing CIA badge. It's a very heavy-handed way to dispose of a badge, but that's probably why they did it at night. The spin-off is a warning to you that they can get pretty annoyed."

"And I suppose they don't really want to jeopardise their outsourcing gig with US DoD, either." Said Jake,

"Correct, " said Chuck, " although I'm wondering if there is also a sleeping partner involved? Some sort of further link back to Raven?"

"It would make sense, " said Christina, " And also explains this kind of extreme action. It's unusual nowadays to be flagrantly throwing bombs around on another nation's soil unless you want to be classified as a terrorist."

Christina added, " This was a clean operation, they did it the way we would. Quiet, tap the glass with a hammer, throw in an incendiary grenade and be away before it's even exploded. It is almost textbook. They'll have used a moped too, to get away. An automatic disguise with the crash-helmet and leathers. Probably a black-painted bike as well."

Chuck nodded as the other looked towards Christina. Chuck began to realise how she got the name Archangel.

"What are we going to do about the office then?" asked Clare.

Bigsy was sitting quietly tapping something into a laptop.

"I've found the perimeter video, " he said, " Two people, in leathers, on a motorcycle. They came along the road by the back of the building and then turned onto the front. Yes, a small hammer. It is just like Christina said."

"How far does that video go back?" asked Christina.

"Well, we should have about two weeks of it in a kind of endless loop. It only starts up when there's movement, " answered Bigsy.

"We'll need to go through it then, " said Christina, " Look for anyone loitering or looking suspicious - particularly in the last couple of days."

"Good thinking, " said Chuck, " They must have scoped the place in advance."

"They also seemed to know where to throw the grenade, " said Christina, " Although it's so powerful I guess anywhere inside would work."

"The irony is, they didn't get the badge, " said Bigsy, " It's still in my backpack. I never got around to transferring it."

"A lead then!" said Christina, " What's his name?"

"Her name, " said Bigsy, " Although I'll need to fish it out to remember, she was badged as CIA."

"*Chertovskiy!* We can take this head on, " said Christina. Chuck looked over to Christina, in a whole different way.

Jake interrupted, " I've spoken to the insurance people today and they will want to send someone around. To check if it really was fire damage. If so, then I think we'll get money to make good. If they sense foul play, I don't think they will want to pay anything, or it will, at least go on for ages."

"Okay, " said Christina, " I think I should go back to your offices this afternoon. We can make this job a whole lot easier for them."

"They said not to touch anything, " said Jake.

"No, of course, " said Christina, " But first I'll be making a side trip to B&Q."

"I'm coming too, " said Bigsy, " What's the opposite of frightened?"

The clean-up

Bigsy and Christina spent the afternoon at the Triangle offices. Christina seemed to know what she was doing as she carefully re-arranged a few pieces from the incendiary. She had insisted that Bigsy and her wear full DIY overalls inside, so they looked like something out of a crime scene or a science fiction thriller.

"This gear was so hard to come by during that viral infection, " said Bigsy, " And now we can get it at builders' merchants."

They had not gone to B&Q in the end, instead to a firm by the side of a railway bridge near to Borough Market. Bigsy had known it and was right that they seemed to stock everything that Christina needed. Overalls, goggles, brushes, cleaner fluid, paint, sand, rubber gloves, talcum powder.

"We just need a few makeup essentials now, " said Christina, pointing towards London Bridge station, "Trust me."

Bigsy had watched Christina at work. She'd poured the bleach onto the floor and let it run. She'd dropped various makeup items into the epicentre of the fire and set fire to a small carrier bag.

She'd switched on an office fan and let it blow talcum powder all over the room. Bigsy was coughing.

"That should be enough, " said Christina, " we've contaminated the scene well enough for any investigator to be confused now. See the epicentre is now a bag of cosmetics, which have caught fire and melted everywhere." There's new dust over everything from the talcum powder and I've left the container inside the melted plastic bag."

"What about the bleach?" asked Bigsy.

"Silly you, keeping a supply of bleach in the back of one of those metal filing cabinets. It must have burst and run out all over the floor."

Bigsy smiled, And the source of it all?

"A hot socket, " said Christina. "Look, this one here."

She pointed to where a desk light had been connected to a wall socket. She showed Bigsy the burnt wiring.

"See, faulty wiring in this old property, she said, " There's no way that you could know about it. When the inspector comes around we might have to help him find this, " she said, rather pointedly.

"And the broken window?" asked Bigsy.

"We should ride that one, " said Christina, "It could have been broken by the firemen. Fixing it will look way more suspicious."

I don't think I've ever been to a wrecked building to tidy up in quite this way, before, " said Bigsy.

"I studied a whole unit on it, back in Russia, " said Christina.

Anne-Maria Bristow

'Anne-Marie Bristow', it said, 'CIA Field Agent.'

They had all agreed to meet in Chuck's hotel room. He had offered it because it was so large. They had ordered some room service and were eating and drinking.

"We need to run a sting on that Field Operation out in East London, " said Christina, " I'm thinking of going with Clare this time."

"No offence, " Bigsy, " But I think we need to try another angle."

"Okay, none taken, " said Bigsy, " but why would you take Clare along?"

"Well, we read one another, " said Christina, " And she is kinda hot."

Chuck looked up, " I sense trouble brewing, " he said.

"Not exactly, " said Christina, " But I think we can put the frighteners onto Anne-Marie Bristow."

"Imagine if two FSB agents turn up at your front desk? Imagine if you are compromised as the one that gave the whole station away?"

"I think Anne Marie is going to want listen to us."

"Especially if one of us can talk like an FSB agent and the other one looks just like one, "

"Okay, " said Clare, " So I'm the one in a leather trench coat and dark glasses?"

She looked at Christina.

"No, too obvious, we'll dress you to look like a recognisable agent. I have just the person in mind, although you will need a ginger wig."

Christina moved over to Bigsy's computer.

"Type in Anna Chapman, " she said, " She's a spies' spy."

"Hah, " said Chuck, " She was traded back a few years ago I seem to remember, "

"That's right, but it was something like a 10 for 4 swap. She's the real deal, a honey trap who worked her way into high places. She even allegedly hired the now discredited Max Clifford to help zigzag her way out of accusations." Said Christina, " She was something of a legend with us, because she managed to keep her real name through just about all of it. And she wasn't field trained like we all are. She just spoke the languages and allegedly flaunted herself around the clubs."

Bigsy came back, " Here we are, here you are - you read

it, Christina…"

Christina continued: "А́нна Васи́льевна Ча́пман, (That's Anna Chapman) born Anna *Vasil'yevna Kushchyenko* is a Russian intelligence agent, media personality, and model who was arrested in the United States as part of the Illegals Program spy ring.

At the time of her arrest she was accused of espionage on behalf of the Russian Federation's external intelligence agency, the *Sluzhba vneshney razvedki*. She had previously gained British citizenship through marriage, which she used to gain residency in the U.S.

"Em, am I supposed to be learning from this character profile?" asked Clare.

"Well, it says here that she was a catwalk model too and had her own TV show. She even had a UK passport, although that was revoked."

"Well, she's certainly hot, " said Bigsy, " I just found the Russian cover of Maxim, where she seems to be wearing Agent Provocateur lingerie, "

"Let me see, " said Jake, " Oh, yes, " he said, " I see what you mean, but what about that one with the chains, or that one with the red gloves? - What do we think? I'd say 10."

"Boys, " said Christina, " Concentrate! We need enough of the character of her to make Anne-Marie Bristow think Anna Chapman is back in town…And anyway look, this one of her posing with a Kalashnikov, she's holding it all wrong."

"Let's see, now, " said Bigsy, " However improbable this is, she seems to own a clothing fashion line as well. Should we dress Clare in some of the Anna Chapman line?"

Christina and Clare looked. They both shook their heads. "No, not good enough, they really don't look all that great, " said Christina, " and I don't think they would suit Clare either."

Clare looked around, " I'm not sure I like this idea, being dressed by committee, " she said.

"I agree, " said Christina, " Let's go to my apartment, we can discuss it between the two of us."

The others nodded, Jake leaned over to Bigsy and said, " Send me that link, would you?"

Snake-look leather belt

Clare and Christina were back at Christina's flat. They had poured a cool wine.

"How will you be with a wig?" asked Christina, " I'll admit I'm so used to it now that I don't even think about it."

"I reckon I could do it, " said Clare. "It's good then that we've come back to mine, " said Christina, " I've a few of the accessories tucked away here, "

She pulled out a large plastic crate from under the bed.

"Wow, party equipped!" said Clare.

"Less need for all of this, nowadays, " said Christina, " But I think we can use some of it for you."

"Look, we'll see if we can find some more pictures of her,"

They looked on the internet, but many of the pictures were of Anna in swimwear.

"I forget about all of the British tabloids sometimes, " said Christina, " Ready to exploit the female form."

"How about these?" said Clare, " It looks as if it is from a catwalk shoot."

"Excellent, " said Christina, " These are more like her day clothes, "

They both looked at the pictures. "This one, " said Clare, " Ironic that she is carrying a gun in it?"

"Do you think you could pull off that look? I think you could! It's a killer!" said Christina.

They studied it some more.

"Go on then, " said Clare, " Let's give it a go!"

Christina found a small leather jacket, complete with a faux fur collar. "There, " she said, " The first building block!"

"…And a wig, something like this one!" with a flourish she produced a shoulder length ginger wig.

Clare looked at it, pensively.

"No. No. We'll get you your own one!" said Christina, " You won't have to borrow mine!"

"Now we need some tight black leggings. Then a brown metallic top, and a wide, brown snake-look leather belt."

"And makeup? - That pale pink lipstick…" tailed off Christina.

"Shopping?" said Clare, " Shopping!" said Christina, " We are close enough to Sloane Square around here."

"Okay, let's hit it, " said Clare.

Listening Station

Although the Masons are not implicated as an organization in CIA and military mind control, connections in the network of doctors were maintained in part through high rank Masons.

— Colin A. Ross, The C.I.A. Doctors: Human Rights Violations by American Psychiatrists

Magpie

Christina and Clare were busy. They found the clothes, including a different snakeskin effect leather jacket which just screamed out to be bought.

Then back to Christina's trying it all on.

"Woooow. You look like one badass spy!" said Christina.

Clare looked in the mirror. She hardly recognised herself. She could be that Anna they had all been looking at in the internet pictures.

"Magpie!" said Christina, " You've earned the spy-name now!"

"C'mon, Let's go back to Chuck's."

They took the train. Clare couldn't believe the number of looks she was getting. Christina smiled, " I think you know how to work that look, " she said.

Inside the Mondrian, a couple of the check -in staff came forward, Clare realised that they thought she was someone famous and were trying to be A-list about the service.

"It's okay, " she said, " I'm already here, we are on the 11th floor."

"Would you like us to show you to your room?" asked the concierge.

"Um, that's okay, " answered Clare, then to Christina, " That's a first, being shown to the room when we're already checked in."

"A-list treatment. I expect they are looking you up right now, " said Christina.

They arrived at Chuck's rather elaborate room. Christina had the key and they let themselves in.

"Oh. My. God." Said Jake, " Clare, is that you! Sensational!" Bigsy looked up, " Wow, and that's for both of you by the way. We are in the presence of FSB greatness. Chuck, how could you allow this?"

Chuck looked over and grinned, " Nice work - you two should be able to scare the bejesus out of Anne-Marie. Only thing is, Clare looks a little younger than Anna Chapman"

"You mean younger and hotter, " said Jake.

They were outside of the American Listening Station, in Canada Water.

"Look, " said Christina, " A Wagamama's - perfect. Go get a table there in a minute and say it is for three of us. I'll get Anne-Marie to come outside of the building. It'll be much easier to talk there and gives us options for our getaway."

They walked into the Wagamama's and were shown to a long bench table.

Christina explained to the waiter that she had to go away for a few minutes but then she would be back with a friend. In the meantime, Clare ordered a drink.

Around the corner, Christina went to the Reception desk.

"Hi, I'm here to see Anne-Marie Bristow, but if you could say to her, I think she will prefer to meet me downstairs. My name is Katarina, Katarina Voronin."

"Would you like to be issued with a pass?"

"Oh no, that won't be necessary, perhaps you could simply call her, she knows what it is about."

"Hello, Yes, Ms Bristow, we have a …Ms Voronin here to see you. She says she will meet you downstairs at Reception."

"Yes, Okay, Right…She will be downstairs in about five minutes to meet you."

Christina thought to herself that she hoped that Anne-Marie looked like her pass card picture.

Christina looked around the lobby. There were no obvious signs of people closing in on her. She could see the ceiling cameras, none of them had adjusted focus towards her.

She had made the request seem innocuous enough. For a moment she wondered if Voronin had been a good choice of alias. It was the most intimidating, so long as they looked it up afterwards. She hoped that Ann-Marie didn't have as good a memory as Chuck.

Then, a few moments later, a youngish woman walked up to the reception desk. Christina guessed that she was maybe 22-23 years old.

"Hello, I'm here to meet Ms Varranan?" she said.

"Excellent, " thought Christina, " she hasn't heard of Katrina Voronin."

"Hello Anne-Marie, I'm Katarina. I've something to discuss with you but it's better that we pop outside. I've a table at Wagamama's. It is around lunch time."

"Oh, hello Katarina! I'm pleased to meet you. It all sounds very mysterious. Can I ask what it is about?"

"Look, " whispered Christine, " I don't want to get you into trouble, but I think I might have found something of yours."

"Oh, " said Anne-Marie, " I see, well in that case I'll be pleased to join you."

She looked over to the desk and called "Thank you, " Christina looked and did the same and they walked towards the double doors that led out onto the pavement.

"Thank you for agreeing to see me, " said Christina, " Only I think we have something belonging to you. We were aware that you might get into trouble if we handed it in in your lobby or posted it back."

"It's my badge, I assume?" said Marie-Anne, " I did get into some trouble actually, but they still issued me with another one. They said that if I found it I should hand it back. They are hoping I will find it, in any case."

They were already at the doors of Wagamama's. They stepped inside and the same waiter showed them to the table with Clare.

"This is my friend Anna, " said Christina.

"Hello Anna - but I guess you know my name already." Clare noticed that Anne-Marie checked her longer than was necessary. She assumed it was the outfit.

"Yes, now here is the thing. We are not just two nice strangers, " said Christina.

"We are both working for Russian intelligence. For *Sluzhba vneshney razvedki* - The SVR. Your pass card has given us insights into the work being conducted at your building in Canada Water. In fact, you could say that other of our identities are a State Secret. Unlike yours, which you seem to have accidentally given to a foreign power."

Christina looked at Anne-Marie. She seems to be close to tears. Clare also noticed.

"Look, " said Clare, " We really don't want to get you into trouble, but we'll want a little help in return."

"No this can't be happening to me, " said Anne Marie, " I just wanted a life less ordinary than in Washington. My parents were all for me making a jump from the Homeland to somewhere foreign. I'd no idea that the English spoke a different language from we Americans."

"This is very simple, " said Christina, " This is a one-time deal. One time and we will be gone forever. You have my word on that and you can check me in the files when you get back if you don't believe me."

"We want to know what you are doing and who is running you in that Listening Station, " said Clare.

Anne-Marie sniffed and wiped her face with the paper serviette.

The server appeared, " Is everything all right?" he asked noticing Anne-Marie's crestfallen face.

"It's fine, " said Christina, " Our friend here just heard some bad news. Clare why don't you order for us all?"

"Vegetarian?" asked Clare, looking at Anne-Marie.

"No, thank you, " replied Anne-Marie.

Clare looked to the waiter and said, "In that case we'll have a chicken nikko with white rice, shirodashi ramen and teriyaki lamb and a bottle of chenin blanc cherry tree hill. We'll share everything."

Christina and Anne-Marie were both impressed that Clare could invent a selection so quickly, but then Christina remembered that Clare had been waiting for them for around ten minutes.

"So, you'll understand that we are offering to make this entire situation go away in return for a little information. You won't see us ever again, nor anyone else from the FSB in conjunction with this."

"We also know that you are supposed to log agent contact to the CIA, but rest assured we have made sure we are untraceable. If you log us, you'll only be drawing attention to yourselves."

"Why me?" asked Anne-Marie, " I've no status or profile in Minerva."

"That's the point, " said Christina, " FSB targeted you because you are below suspicion."

"It's simple, " said Clare, " You just need to tell us some things about the station and we'll be on our way and you'll have your pass back. By the time you've eaten the ramen, all of this will be over."

As if on cue, the first of the dishes arrived, with the bottle of wine. The server poured three glasses of wine and they set the bowl in the middle where each of them could pick at it.

"We need some side plates too, " asked Clare.

"I don't want to make this difficult, " said Anne-Marie, " But I don't think I know anything. The main operation is outsourced to Qube and seems to be a boiler house scam, in any case. I'm worried enough about this getting back to Washington. I dare not tell my parents what I have got into."

Christina actively listened to be able to feed some of what she had heard back into the questions. Clare was quite impressed.

"So, if Minerva is being run by Qube on behalf of the CIA, what are the boiler house scams that are being played?"

"Well, it seems to me that we are mainly tracking British politicians and senior business people. The only one I am aware of is named Bernard Driscoll - I think he is a government minister. Instead of conventional lobbying, they target these people in other ways, to get them complicit. What is the phrase? 'Moral suasion' - I think we millennials call it 'social engineering'.

"Then Qube lobbies the targeted individual for a new deal somewhere or other. Right now it seems to be something to do with Russia and Celarus. I think there is something being positioned."

"So, who is running the station then?" asked Christina, " Is it the CIA?"

Anne-Marie replied, "I thought it was, and that is how I got transferred here." It seems to be run by Qube though and some of us, mainly the more junior ones are being used as a front."

"Look - I don't want any trouble from this, nor for my parents or family. I don't think I have more to say to you though, " she looked long at Christina and Clare was trying to work out what it meant.

Christina looked at Anne-Marie and said, "One day you'll be able to tell the tale of how you met Katarina Voronin and Anna Chapman and were trying to recruit them. You can say that you had discovered that the shot at the GU7 summit in Paris was an attempt by the two of them working together. That you'd spotted them plotting in London and lured them into a trap. Christina pulled out her iPhone and instantly snapped a selfie of the three of them together.

"When we are long gone from here, I will send you this picture. You can do with it what you will, just make sure you use it to enhance your reputation. It's a tough life being in espionage, especially for a woman."

"Respect, " said Clare.

"Uvazhat', " said Christina.

"Thank you, " said a somewhat dazed Anne-Marie.

"Now here is your pass; remember we are two bad-ass ladies, so don't even think about double crossing us. Take a few minutes to walk around outside, then head back in as if nothing has happened.

"Don't take that pass in for a couple more days and if I were you, I'd find it somewhere inside the building, wedged under some paper on your desk or something. That way people will think it's just a silly mistake."

"Waiter, " called Clare and settled the bill.

"Okay let's all be on our way, " said Christina.

Young

"My god, " said Christina, " Anna-Marie was young!"

"Yes, I wasn't expecting that, " agreed Clare.

"I think we've scared her half to death, " said Christina.

"When she started talking about her parents and her family", said Christina, " She'll be back at the office looking us both up. She'll find Katarina Voronin and Anna Chapman, that's for sure."

"It'll probably start a whole new search for Anna around London, " said Clare, " You know, I think I'll miss her!"

They both smiled. "Now we've got to tell the boys what happened, " said Christina.
…

Back at the Mondrian, Chuck's suite had begun to take on the look of the Triangle office. Bigsy had 'just' added a few cables and boxes and there seemed to now be a printer as well.

"You can have stuff from Amazon delivered to a hotel

room, as long as you're a high enough status of customer, " said Bigsy.

Chuck didn't seem to mind, as long as they kept the mess in his annex room, which was next to the main bedroom with its balcony.

"So, what happened?" asked Chuck, " Oh and well done, by the way!"

"It is some kind of set-up,' said Christina. "No wonder they were angry that we'd managed to infiltrate their premises. It seems as if the CIA originally set this up, but for whatever reason passed the running of it over to Qube. It's an outsourced listening station as we guessed. They've got some young CIA agents in to front everything; they are effectively interns, judging by the one we met. Then they are using the station - it's called Minerva - by the way - yes they are using it to pressurise various UK politicos and business people."

Clare continued, " Anne-Marie described it as like 'boiler room'. You know those scams where they keep calling old people and trying to trick them out of their money. Except in this case the boiler room plotting is targeting MPs and the like. I guess it's faster than lobbying.

Clare added, " Actually, Anne-Marie sounded pretty hacked off about the whole thing. She said she had moved from Washington DC. She was probably on a fast track over there. I guess you must do some international work to get further but then she is stuck with a seedy scam. Worse than that, she then gets compromised by two Russian agents, who she later discovers to have top profiles.

"It's not exactly her week. And all because of light fingers here, " She looked over to Bigsy.

"I'll try running Minerva as a codeword to see if it lights up anywhere, " said Chuck.

"Now, ever so politely, you may leave all your contraptions here, but I'd like to ask you all to leave until tomorrow morning, if I may." Chuck smiled and the others smiled back.

"Oh, it would be lovely to have an office with air-conditioning, room service and a view of the Thames, " said Bigsy

"Welcome to my world" said Chuck, eyeing the clock. Amanda would be back soon.

Blackbird calling

Christina's cell phone rang. It was the dead of night and she was back at her flat.

"Hello?" she answered.

"Archangel? It's Blackbird. We need to talk."

"Sure, by this line or in another way?" asked Christina, noticing that the number was from overseas, although she did not recognise the dialling code.

"This way is good, " said Blackbird, " Encrypted and VPN - Look, we've found out that someone may be looking for you."

"Who?" asked Christina, " I thought I'd covered my tracks pretty well."

"Yes, but this is someone you already know - Chuck Manners from the US Government. He normally operates as Black Ops - blowing things up - shooting things down. This time we think he has been tasked with finding you."

"So, do I need to move?" asked Christina. She did not want to give away that Chuck and she had already met.

"And do you know where he is?" she asked.

"We think he is in London; we are sending a couple of agents to find him - *аук и тупик* - They are a man and woman team from the Academy. The agents are already based in London, so they should be there almost immediately."

"How is Antanov?"

"Antanov is safely back to his home and family."

"There's something else: The other thing we have picked up is some chatter about a new US station somewhere in East London. We'd like you to see if you can find out anything."

Christina thought it interesting that Minerva Station was now breaking cover. Perhaps the bombing of the Triangle Offices had created the leak?

Vauxhall Cross

The next morning, Amanda was back in her SI6 office in Vauxhall Cross. She had filed a report about the Minerva Listening Station and another about Qube but had held off filing anything about Driscoll.

Even in SI6 she knew that the walls could have ears and that anything about Driscoll would be likely to get back to him.

By the afternoon, she was engrossed in another situation, when the phone rang.

"Hi Amanda, its Grace from GCHQ - I think I've found something."

"Hi Grace, it sounds intriguing, what is this about?" she asked.

"It's an interesting development, " Grace said, " We paid attention to that Listening Station you found out at Canada Water. You know, the one called Minerva. Your source was right, it is a boiler room.

Grace continued, "Several MPs are being approached, so it's doing the work of a lobbying machine, but without the usual detection and declarations."

"They seem to be operating it through some typical slush and sleaze approaches to the MPs and other company officials, " she said.

"For some, it's money, for others access to events and for a few - ahem -'Favours'

"It's a clever system though, because they can masquerade as CIA or MI6 while they are luring people into the snare. And there seems to be some level of additional secrecy applied by appearing as the secretive brotherhood of Freemasons."

"It's hard to pin it down, though. It seems to be operating as an outsourcer through the military contractor called Qube."

Grace continued, " I checked on Qube too, it's a subsidiary of Raven, and they have been mostly operating out of the US. They seem to get attached to any peacekeeping deals as quasi-militia and then, through Raven contracts, supply food, laundry, transportation and other life-cycle management services.

"It's notable that Raven has made its name in oil and energy provisioning and it doesn't seem to mind skating close to the edge. For example, it supplied four pulse neutron generators to Sudan after the US ceasefire. There's no match between funding and the supply of these devices, and it's not clear where Sudan would expect to get the foreign funds to buy one, let alone four of the devices."

"It smacks of baksheesh, " said Amanda.

"I'd say so, it looks like bribery on an industrial scale, " said Grace.

"But we are not sure who is running them?" asked Amanda.

Grace continued, " Well it's not us, and I don't think it is the CIA. I can't be definite about this, but if I had to guess for someone, then I'd point towards corporate corruption. Probably Raven permitting the operation of this through their subsidiaries."

She paused and then said, " I've been thinking about it. Raven have got most of the same capabilities as a nation state. Funding, R&D, manufacturing, run-rate production of energy, security forces, espionage and access to powerful people. It's like a pocket state."

Amanda considered what they had found. A corporation wielding state-like levels of influence and bridging political and geographic divides.

"We need to tread carefully with this, " said Amanda to Grace, " If we hint that we know what is happening it could trip some large-scale retribution."

"My thoughts too, " said Grace, " Once I'd realised that Minerva Station could be part of something huge, I pulled my own resources from the investigation. For the last couple of days, I have been working on this alone. And believe me, I've been hidden away underground inside the Core here at Cheltenham."

Chairman of the Board

Fortitude, Prudence, Temperance, Justice

Raven Board Meeting

Sir Charles Frobisher was attending the Raven's board meeting. He had brought another two experts on divestment with him Han Yoon and Brittany Krasnigor.

"They are both from Smooth Pebble, A Venture Capital company, based in Sand Lake Road, Palo Alto, " he said, introducing them to the room.

Han Yoon began, "Hi, my name is Han Yoon, we've a short session on divestment, to help Position Raven's latest move. Sir Charles has asked us along, because you'll want to put some small company thinking into your next big move.

As "Mark Twain put it: What gets us into trouble is not what we don't know. It's what we know for sure that just ain't so."

Han Yoon continued, " So we are here to position a few ideas. There is some PowerPoint as wallpaper behind the session, but we'd like you to take in the main ideas. And

Charles asked us to challenge you all, so don't be shy!"

Brittany took over. She could see the attendees noticing the way she wore her tight-fitting blue dress with the tiniest sleeves and a high neckline. No jewellery, although some high-heeled computer patterned black-and-white shoes.

"The essence of commitment is making a decision. The Latin root for decision is to 'cut away from,' as in an incision. When you commit to something, you are cutting away all your other possibilities, all your other options. - That's what you are here today, deciding. About making that divestment."

She flicked the PowerPoint to a new slide. A picture of a fox and a hedgehog.

"You all know this picture, " she said, " It's a reference to 'Good to Great' by the well-known advisor Jim Collins, " But let's not forget that the wisdom is much older; "The fox knows many things; the hedgehog knows one big thing." That was Archilochus, Greek philosopher in 8th century BC."

"Can I stop you there?" said one of the Board, " I'm Bob Jones, Head of Acquisitions. This kind of strategizing wizardry might go down well in sunny California, but here we need practical advice and action."

"Okay then, you decide, " said Brittany, " I can take this up a notch. Let's look at the specifics of divestment."

Sir Charles intervened, " Please continue Brittany, but if you can get to the specifics, that would be wonderful."

She flipped through the slides to one entitled:

'Smart Divest'

"Okay, " she said, " Let's get to a few rules:

"1) Dedicate a team to divestment full-time, just as you do with acquisitions."

She could see they were still looking at her dress.

"2) Establish objective criteria for determining divestment candidates—don't panic and sell for a song in bad times."

A couple of them were doodling.

"3) Work through all the details of the de-integration process before you divest."

One was looking at his smartphone.

"4) Make sure you can clearly articulate how the deal will benefit the buyer and how you will motivate the unit's employees to stay on until the deal is done."

One of the doodles was a picture of her shoes.

"So, can I ask? Do you already have a framework like this in place?" asked Brittany.

"Absolutely, " said Bob Jones, " We have regular sessions to track process using a Red/Amber/Green tracker. As of now, we have - er... 17 Red. 14 Amber and 27 Green category items."

"That's great, " said Brittany, " but what happens when you miss a milestone or a target? - Why are you needing to use the Red Category so much?"

"Yes, " said Sir Charles, " We do seem to have quite a few Red items on the list? William, any comment?"

William Daniels, Head of Operations answered, " Well, we are pushing the line along, flattening the curve, getting rid of the lumps. It's a multi-dimensional situation. We have to matrix manage the situation across different business lines."

Brittany challenged, " But doesn't it look a little bit like a long straight line of green and then a suspicious bulge of Amber and Red? If this was a carpet, you'd have swept most things underneath, but then pushed them all into a big heap in the middle?"

Now it was William's turn to look aggrieved, " You misunderstand our process. We are able to track all of the critical events and put something in place to get on top of them."

"But how does that show up?" asked Brittany, " Slippage? deferral? What was your original timeline?"

Sir Charles spoke up again, " Yes, this project has slipped. There seem to be several areas that almost don't seem very keen to see it go ahead. It's almost as if they are trying to block it."

"Organisational Antibodies, " said Brittany, " They are the people who will feel threatened by the outcome from the divestment. People with comfortable positional power who are keen to see the initiative flounder."

Now it was Bob's turn again, " I don't think any of us are trying to stop this, you know, we, the Board are pushing for this to take place."

"So, is there a dedicated team?" asked Han Yoon.

A moment's silence.

"We are the dedicated team, driving this from the Board," answered Bob.

"Bluntly then, where's the single throat to choke if it all goes wrong?" countered Han Yoon.

They looked around the table. A younger looking attendee was scribbling furiously onto an iPad.

"I think Han Yoon has got a point, " said Sir Charles, " We should really have set up a specific team for this."

Brittany continued, " Used consistently, the four steps I outlined create disciplines to produce an internal sell-side capability that enables divestors to generate superior returns for their shareholders.

"Most firms - I'm sure you are included - You have sizeable corporate development organisations, elaborate acquisition pipelines, and extensive relationships with investment banks, which all drive buy-side activity.

"She looked around, several of the attendees were taking notes. The younger looking attendee was still scribbling earnestly on his iPad.

"In fact, as more companies—particularly the type we deal with - private equity firms—have focused on deal-making disciplines, buy-side returns have improved over the past few years.

"That's all very well, but your outfit tends to deal with smaller organisations. Raven is very large, more than your entire portfolio of companies, " said Bob.

"I might agree with your numbers, but you miss a point, " said Brittany, " The best divestors approach divestitures with the same level of planning and rigour that their counterparts in corporate development bring to acquisitions.

Brittany continued, " They have established sell-side teams, which are constantly screening their company's portfolio for divestiture candidates and are continually thinking through the timing and implementation steps needed to maximize value."

"Well we know which area we want to divest, and why, " said William.

"William is right, " said Charles, " There are special circumstances to our planned divestment. It is just that not everyone can yet see the advantages."

Han Yoon cut back in, " Obviously, it makes the most sense to sell a business while potential acquirers can still extract value from the operations and take steps to reignite profitable growth.

"Yet our observation is that when faced with the reality of a divestment many companies blow it. They hesitate yet are unable to support the level of investment required to transform the business. These companies hold on, often for many years, until the unit has lost much of the value it once had."

"Exactly, " said Sir Charles, " And we are hoping that the divested company will have considerable up-side once established."

"Hello, I'm Lucy Sidwell, from Corporate Treasury. You talk about up-side, but surely that only affects the divested company?"

"Not quite, " said Brittany, " If you can prove the multiple in a new business, then it can be factored into the sale price. You could even incorporate a share trade as part of the deal."

"But let us move on to the Plan for De-Integration. Once you, the board and the senior executives have decided to divest a unit, they must determine what type of separation will best meet the company's needs and then carefully think through the implementation steps required to generate the maximum value from the separation."

"Bob, has that been strategized by your unit? And William, do you have a tracker for those elements of the plan? You can see that without the two key building blocks you will have an opportunity for the institutional antibodies - the resistors - get a foothold."

"That's where a Force Field Analysis could be worthwhile, " added Han Yoon, "List your top people and identify whether they are for or against the divestment. See who can be converted, but as importantly, those people that need to be reassigned.

Sometimes they are called 'the saboteurs'."

There was some shuffling of chairs after Han Yoon's last comment.

"I said we'd bring in these folks to challenge us. It's certainly giving us something to consider, " said Sir Charles.

"We need to talk about something that Lucy will be interested in, " said Brittany, " We need to make the separation pay. Corporations are not private-equity firms—they are not in the business of buying and selling assets. But they need to be just as savvy about how to structure a divestiture deal and whom to sell to. Here's the best thinking about the "how" and the "who" of divesting."

"Yes, that's right, and we mentioned it earlier, " said Han Yoon, "Once a company has decided that a unit is not vital to its core, it must determine how best to separate it out. That involves answering two important questions - cash or stock? And, all of it or part of it?

"In most cases, selling a business for cash makes the most sense. There are instances, however, when spinning off a division to shareholders can be a better bet—either because the seller has no use for the cash proceeds (and doesn't want to hold them for fear of becoming a takeover target) or because a spin-off would produce higher after-tax proceeds."

"Most of the time, it's easier to sell a whole business than to break it up into pieces, keeping some and selling others. In some cases, though, selling the whole business is not desirable or not feasible."

Brittany continued, " And, of course there is the important question of who will the buyer be? A couple of straightforward questions, I'm sure they are in your list, Bob?"

Bob remained silent. Brittany could see that he was annoyed at being outplayed by her, as presenter.

"First question: Who will pay the highest price? Typically, the company that makes the best offer is the one that views the property as the most strategic. But sellers cannot assume that buyers will intuitively understand their own strategic advantages, nor can sellers count on investment banks to tout the deal's potential effectively. The key to maximising the sale price is seeing the divested business through the buyer's eyes and tailoring the sales pitch accordingly. This "reverse due diligence" extends to identifying and quantifying potential cost and revenue synergies for potential buyers."

"Second Question: Is one buyer better than another from a strategic standpoint? In most cases, selling to the highest bidder will create the highest value for the divestor's shareholders. But not always. Divestors must be careful to account for the competitive threat posed by each potential buyer."

Sir Charles said, " I think we've sorted this questions out, haven't we?" He looked around the table. He sensed he could cut the atmosphere with a knife.

"William? Are we okay with this? Or do you haven additional comments?"

William muttered, " No, it's fine."

"What about you Bob?"

"If I'm honest, I think our own strategy team has laid out most of what Ms. Krasnigor is saying. I'm not sure any of it is new to us."

"Lucy? How about you?" asked Sir Charles.

"I'd like to hear something about the compelling logic of the deal. People like to ask 'What's In It For Me? – What's in it for Buyers and Employees?" answered Lucy.

Brittany answered, " Yes Lucy, you make a great point. The best divestors clearly communicate what's in the deal for all involved. This entails having convincing—and honest—answers to four questions:

"First: What actions should be taken to improve the profitability of the divestiture candidate or fuel its growth?"

Brittany realised the scribbler with the iPad had been selected as a minute-taker. She thought now would be a good time to say, " Er, don't worry to take notes. I've a presentation pack which I can send you across.

She continued, " Second: How long will it take the buyer to achieve the deal's full potential value? (The faster an acquirer can realize the increase in value, the more it will be willing to pay for the divested business.)"

Those two at the far end of the table were still staring at her dress.

"Third: How should the value that can be unlocked through divestiture be split between the buyer and the seller?

She clapped her hands together. The two starers both looked startled.

"Finally: How will we motivate and inspire the people in the business to keep it humming along until the deal closes (and beyond)?"

Brittany sat down, " Look, I think I've unpacked enough, and I can tell you were engaged and thinking about this during my talk. It's refreshing to know that Bob, William and Lucy have already got many of these points covered. I'd still recommend that you set up a separate team, but at least you know where you are heading with this."

Sir Charles spoke, " Well, I'd like to thank Smooth Pebble for their insights into our divesture and they have certainly given us food for thought. Let us hope our plans skim along the lake now- like a smooth pebble, rather than sink into it."

Dorothy, could you please show Han Yoon and Brittany Krasnigor back to my office now, and offer them some refreshments.

"Now, Next Item."

Grace Cathedral Hill

Dorothy showed Han Yoon and Brittany Krasnigor into the annex to Sir Charles' office.

They sat waiting for his return, but both keep quiet.

Around fifteen minutes later, Sir Charles returned,
" Sorry, we had a few things to wrap up in that meeting after you'd left. I can see that Dorothy has made sure you have some coffee. Come on into my office."

"What did you think?" asked Sir Charles, as he walked across to a small meeting table.

"I'm not sure that they were that pleased to see us, " said Han Yoon.

"I think you rattled their cages somewhat. Thank you - that was exactly what I asked you to do. To draw out their positions."

"We it is clear to me that Bob Jones wasn't a team player, " said Brittany, " He seemed very antagonistic, almost to justify his position."

"Yes, he is fond of asking questions like, 'what do we mean by analyse?' or 'what do we mean by 'strategy'? As a way to slow down the debate, he seemed to be doing it with you two, " said Sir Charles, " I'm afraid he may have to go."

"Then William. He was on top of a process, but it wasn't the right one, " said Tiffany, " It all looks business-like, but he's missed the main point, "

Sir Charles replied, " Yes I get snowed with diagrams and Excel charts from his department, but they never tell what is going along."

"I actually thought Lucy came up with couple of good questions, " said Brittany.

"I agree, said Han Yoon, " She seems to be treating it like a VC project and was following the money."

"Yes, Lucy is quite an asset to us here. Do you think I should move her to oversee the divestment project?"

"You could, " said Han Yoon, " But I'm aware of some extraordinary circumstances around this project, from my briefing with Michael Tovey."

"You know Michael…" said Charles, " I was forgetting - of course - he introduced your company to me."

"Yes, and he spelled out to me that you have some special interests running through the divestment, too, " said Han

Yoon, " Look I won't beat about the bush…I might look Asian by descent, but I can still recognise a Masonic handshake."

"Ah yes, I thought the Communist Party had stopped Freemasonry in China?" said Sir Charles.

"Hmm, I'm American, " said Han Yoon, " From San Francisco actually. My Lodge is on Grace Cathedral Hill, opposite the Cathedral, actually. That is how Michael Tovey recommended us, He was in town for a VC thing, and we were both a little hungry, so we went to get hot dog, down the Hyde Street Pier."

Sir Charles frowned, " Yes, that's right, he called me up from San Francisco to recommend you. And he said you were a psychologist by training, Brittany?"

Brittany replied, " That's right, my presentation was designed to push a few buttons, see what kind of response we could get. Nothing fancy, but it seemed to work! And they never did ask about the hedgehog! "

Sir Charles said, " I think I know the answer - the fox is a cunning creature, able to devise a myriad of strategies for sneak attacks upon the hedgehog…Fast, sleek, beautiful, fleet of foot, and crafty – the fox looks like the sure winner.

"The hedgehog on the other hand, is a dowdier creature…He waddles along, going about his simple day, searching for lunch and taking care of his home…(but) despite the greater cunning of the fox, the hedgehog always wins. Roadkill excepted, of course."

"That's not bad, " said Brittany, " I won't give you the full answer now - not about that, anyway. But Lucy, yes, she could make a great PM for the divestment, except, as Han Yoon says, if you expect it to be Freemason-inspired."

Fake 'n ham

Bigsy was studying Bernard Driscoll's biography. He had found the entry in Wikipedia and was comparing it with a hatchet piece he'd found in the Guardian.

"Bernard Driscoll has a small semi-detached in Ilford. He has had to flip it a couple of times with his bigger house out in the East Anglian countryside. It would be too embarrassing to reveal Fakenham as his residence and the tax relief and expenses available for the other property was so useful."

"Ha, Fakenham - you can't make it up!" sniggered Jake.

"Driscoll briefly joined the Labour Party in 1983 in Norwich but has stated that by the time he left to go to Reading University he was a Conservative."

"So, he flips in more ways than one!"

Bigsy read further, " Driscoll joined the Reading University Conservative Association and was secretary of Norwich North Young Conservatives. It says he helped to write speeches for Cabinet and Shadow Cabinet ministers, although it doesn't mention which ones."

"What's the quote, said Clare, " 'If you are not a liberal when you're 25, you have no heart. If you are not a conservative by the time you're 35, you have no brain.' "

"Now, now, play nice Clare, " said Jake, laughing.

Bigsy continued, " When applying for a job at the Conservative Research Department he was told he was "insufficiently political" and "insufficiently Conservative", so he turned to journalism.

"All round, a bit useless then?" commented Clare.

Bigsy read, " Then close to home, he worked on the Norfolk Journal in Norwich, where he spent several months on strike in the 1989–1990 dispute over union recognition and representation.

"He got paid, though. It wasn't furlough pay exactly, but he took some sort of union position while the strike was running. A hired gun approach.

"During this time, he wrote a sympathetic biography of a couple of leading lights in the Tory party but was criticised when the books were released for using a ghost writer.

"I remember that, " said Jake, " That ghost writer went on to become a famous author, and in later interviews was asked about the Driscoll time. I think he said Driscoll was entirely 'hands-off" for the books and didn't really care for one of the politicians either. I think later Driscoll even got into some trouble about things that were included in the book."

Bigsy continued, " His pre-political career is interesting in that it suffered from the 'two-year problem', where he would only do anything for a couple of years before being asked to leave. It was symptomatic of someone that wasn't particularly good at anything but was given the benefit of the doubt after the first year's lame results but then went on to confirm the reservations in the second year."

"Oh yes, " said Clare, " We've all met people like that."

Bigsy continued, " Well, then Driscoll somehow inveigled his way to a position at Policy Exchange, a conservative think tank launched in 2002. He was also involved in founding the right-leaning magazine Particulars, to which he occasionally contributes. He was trying to build his credential as a thinker during this period."

Clare said, " The arrogance of the man. I mainly know of him from his tirades against women in the House of Commons. Using a kind of pompous bullying tactic. Thinks he's got a Headmaster power over everyone. I pity his poor wife."

Jake added, " Yeah, I remember when I was a journalist, the journos used to call him 'whip-boy'"

Bigsy continued, " Driscoll expressed admiration in late-February 2003 for New Labour Prime Minister Tony Blair because of the way he was handling the crisis in Iraq: 'As a right-wing polemicist, all I can say looking at Mr Blair now is, what's not to like?' Blair, he thought, was ' behaving like a true Thatcherite'. - It turns out later that the quotes he made were originally attributable to another Tory MP. Oddly enough they have stuck with him as if they were his quotes, right through to his entry on'GoodQuotes.com' "

"As a result, he has almost no followers from within the House, commands no loyalty and is generally reviled. However, he is sitting in a Tory stronghold seat, with a majority of 25,000."

"What about scandals?" asked Jake, " There must be something?"

"No, not really, " said Bigsy, " You can hate him for his policies and his haughty attitude, but he is careful not to get caught. He also has some significant press machinery behind him, retouching anything that looks dubious.

"Here's an example; his swimming-pool in Norfolk needed re-equipping and he put it through as MP expenses. Then we hear how he needs steam therapy for a leg injury that was prescribed by his doctor and that anyway it had been an accounting oversight that he would reimburse in full. The Daily Mail was all over the story and showed Driscoll on crutches, which they said was during the time he couldn't get his routine therapy."

"There's an opinion piece in the Guardian about how Driscoll has reached such roles as Minister, with the thinking that he must somehow have friends in high places."

"So, what have we got?" asked Clare, " A noxious bully narcissist who has access to too much power."

"It seems to be a sign of the times, " said Jake.

Bigsy and Clare nodded.

Berry

Christina arrived at Chuck's hotel suite.

"You must have an infinite budget to keep this going!" she said.

"I seem to get by, " said Chuck, " The spoils of, ahem, Consulting!"

"I know that feeling, " said Christina.

"Yes, I know we are from different sides, but it has been interesting to meet you and to even realise that you are better - than the field reports!" said Chuck.

"I'll take that as a compliment, " smiled Christina, " And I'd like to offer one back - very similar. From one professional to another - I can see you know how to rock the role."

"Come on, come here. A hug, " said Chuck.

They hugged for several seconds.

"If the FSB could see me now!" said Christina, then she changed her tone.

"Look, Chuck, I've some unwelcome news for you, I think..."

Chuck looked suitably serious.

"My handler has been in contact. He was signalling to me that Antanov was safely back in position. But then he gave me some other information. He said that the FSB thought Chuck Manners was in London. That Chuck had got wind that I/Katarina Voronin was in town then he would be on to me."

"Well, we know that isn't the case, " said Chuck relaxing slightly, " If we were going to be fighting it would have started by now and we'd both have small-arms in this room."

Christina giggled.

Chuck realised Christina was armed. "Well, we'd both have small arms pointed at one another!"

"Yes, " said Christina, " So the FSB did what their bureaucracy dictates. They've sent a couple of agents to find you."

"What? I supposed I could have guessed that, " said Chuck, " To be honest, I think I've been having quite a good time here. Amanda, you, the Triangle folk and a really good mystery to resolve."

"Well, I think I'm warning you - much as it saddens me - that it is probably time for you to get the hell out of

Dodge, " said Christina.

"I asked when the two guys were dispatched, and it was over a week ago. I know they will head for Central London and I think I could probably find them easily enough if I went to a couple of the gold-plated clubs in the West End."

"Have you got any names?" asked Chuck, " No just couple of code words. They don't sound very high up though, codenamed *аук и тупик* - auk i tupik - er that's Auk and Puffin.

"What's an Auk?" asked Chuck, bemused.

"I know them quite well, " said Christina, " They look a little like penguins, but are not even related. They spend most of their life at sea."

"So - go on then - tell me - what's your code name, Christina? It'd be useful to know in case I ever hear it in chatter."

Christina hesitated, then said, " It's Archangel."

"No way!" said Chuck. Christina could see the look of astonishment on his face, " I am in the presence of FSB greatness! My god - you have some exploits to your name. I thought Voronin was pretty high up there, but Archangel!"

"It's even *Архангельск* – Arkhangelsk in Russian, " said Christina, " You know something, I'm actually Icelandic, but I was trained in Russia and Bulgaria - this is for you privately, by the way, not for some dossier in the Pentagon. Now you'll have to tell me yours? Come on Colonel Manners."

"Ahem, it's not as good as yours. I'm usually called 'Berry' in dossiers. I've worked under a range of names in missions."

"Berry...wait that's Chuck Berry. I get it, " laughed Christina, " I suppose that's why you've no particular place to go?" she added.

"Not bad for a Russian!" said Chuck.

Christina remembered, " Okay - but as well as their code names, I can tell you that they are a couple; man and woman, who have been running deep cover for several years. Don't think of them as just troublesome though. They are deadly. I think you should move on, get lost again in your own cover. You must have some spare identities? It's time to use one."

Chuck nodded, " Thank you. Thank you, Christina, for this and for your generosity of spirit whilst here with us all. My pledge. If the chips are down, I'll still support you. That's from one professional to another."

"Likewise, " said Christina, " Sometimes it's good to have allies in unusual places., My pledge is also to you."

"Final hugs?" asked Chuck.

"Sure, " said Christina, " Until the next time!"

Occupational hazards

Amanda was back at the Mondrian.

"This is the fourth time I've been to the Mondrian, " said Amanda., " SI6 will begin to show an interest around now."

"What's been your story?" asked Chuck.

"I've told them I have an asset here, but that I don't want to divulge names."

"They are probably already following you, then."

"The operational unit responsible for that is run by Jim Cavendish. He and I have an extensive history. I've told him not to read anything into this. Sorry to say this, Chuck, but I fear we've run our course."

Chuck looked briefly mournful, " No, I understand, " he said. "Occupational hazard of the Life. I've also received a little whisper that I've been spotted by the FSB. I was thinking this would need to be my last day here.

"Give me something to take back, for my story - that I've been talking to an asset, " asked Amanda, " It can be related to that thing you are doing with those Triangle people. You know, the Minerva Station by the Dome."

"Yes, they are on to something. That place may be called Minerva, but it is more like her sister Medusa - you know, the one that could turn people to stone."

"Ah yes, hair of snakes and all that, I remember, " said Amanda.

"Well they seem to have identified that the Triangle team entered their premises and then they used some of the Minerva tracking technology to locate the Triangle offices and send them a message. A big message. Their offices were set on fire. By an American Army incendiary grenade. It isn't obvious to me that there's a direct link, but it is mighty suspicious."

"How can you know it was an American grenade?" asked Amanda.

"Oh, I've seen the evidence, they took part of the canister from the wreckage, photographed it and gave me a copy - it was military grade. An M14, and a very fast operation too. Tap the glass with a hammer, throw the grenade in and exit on a moped. A couple of minutes. Professional and slick. Someone like me did the job. Well, there were two of them on the video clip. A driver and bomber."

"Not entirely a CIA operational style?" said Amanda, " And way too sensitive if caught. Americans throwing bombs around London Streets?"

"I agree, " said Chuck, " They've black-Opp-ed this out. My guess is they didn't need to go far, what with all those Qube security services people around the place."

"That was what The Triangle people thought as well. They decided to go back for a second dig around Qube. It's good for both of us actually because these guys are freelance and clearly not working for UK or US governments. We get deniability, but results."

"This could work out well for both of us, " said Amanda.

Chuck continued, " So they still returned and put the frighteners on one of the CIA workers there. A pretty little thing called Anne-Marie. It sounds as if she got the job through her father's contacts; nothing like fast-tracking it via International assignments."

"However, a couple of the members of the Triangle managed to spook her and she did spill the beans. Minerva is running as a high-class boiler house to scam MPs and senior business players. We think it is cheaper than using lobbyists in a conventional manner and it certainly is stealthier."

"They got a name too, Bernard Driscoll."

"Driscoll, the MP? - Hah, he is too boorish to come up with any serious mischief by himself, they must be using some thick strings to manipulate him! I've had direct dealings with him - a loathsome bullying character and somewhat dim-witted, hiding behind pomposity."

"Well, this might be a chance to see his comeuppance!" said Chuck, " linked with Minerva and something involving Qube."

"Chuck, that is brilliant. I've got a great list of things to take back. Minerva, Driscoll and Qube."

"You know what, you shouldn't be thanking me, you should be thanking those guys that operate as 'The Triangle.'"

"I've noted that too, and I'm intrigued and more than a little bit thankful that you've stayed loyal to them."

"So, the night is yet young? We will have to plan how we extend our friendship when I'm back in D.C."

Chuck gets out of Dodge

The next day, Jake and Bigsy arrived at Chuck's room. Chuck was packed and looked as if he was ready to leave.

"Hi guys, look, I've piled up the equipment that Bigsy brought on the little table in the annex. I think you'll need a large suitcase or something to move it out of the room."

"Chuck - you're leaving. So suddenly too?" said Jake.

"I know, it was always intended to be a flying visit, checking in with a few acquaintances, but ever aware of the possibility that I'd get traced. D'you know that's what's happened, " said Chuck, " I've been put back onto a seek list but the FSB. They've sent a couple of agents to find me."

"What about Christina? She wouldn't do that to you, neither hunt you nor shop you, " said Bigsy.

"No, I agree, I'm certain that Christina was as surprised as anyone. Between you and me, she might just have tipped me off about the situation, " said Chuck.

"I'll be using another identity when I get back to D.C." Said Chuck, " I'm sure we'll all stay connected, in any case."

"Yes, Chuck, it's been pleasure, as always, " said Jake, slapping Chuck on the back.

"Yes, look after yourself and don't be a stranger, " said Bigsy.

"No Clare nor Christina this time, " said Chuck, " Please give them my regards."

For a moment Bigsy and Jake looked awkwardly towards Chuck, but then he said, " Time to haul ass, as we Americans say, "

"Yes, safe travels, " said Bigsy. Jake waved.

Chuck made his way between them, saying, " Oh yes, I've paid for the room tonight, so you've time to move out the gear." And then with a wave, he was gone.

"Wow, that was a turn-up, " said Bigsy. He knew Jake was a good friend of Chuck and of all of them he thought Jake would take Chuck's departure the hardest.

"We'd better move this gear out, " said Jake. Bigsy was already unfolding a couple of large blue IKEA bags from his habitually carried rucksack.

"Yes, if we can put all the small stuff into a couple of these, then one of us can carry the printer and the other one all the junk. If we can get it to the lift, then we can soon move it into a taxi around to mine, " said Bigsy.

"Yes, said Jake, or we could take it to the temporary Regus office that I've got for us."

"Office - that sounds good, said Bigsy, " Whereabouts is it?"

"Central, near the Institute of Directors by Liverpool Street. Ideal for the City of West End and pretty easy commute for all of us - Even Christina. - I thought it would be okay until we either refresh the Triangle Offices or, more likely, find something more modern."

"Cool, " said Bigsy, " When will you tell Clare and Christina?"

"They know already, " said Jake sheepishly, " I told them to go there today instead of coming over here to Chuck's"

"Right, then, " said Bigsy, " What are we waiting for?"

Driscoll Shining

Meet upon the level
Part upon the square

Soft power

Driscoll couldn't believe his luck. Marion had called him after the Formula One dinner. She'd said she was sorry that she had to rush away like that, but she realised that Bernard was caught up in some kind of conversation in any case.

She had asked to meet Driscoll again. This time at Berners Tavern, which Driscoll thought of as an exclusive and showy restaurant.

Marion had explained that ISMC had offered to provide a private dining experience there, but on the understanding that Bernard would take a few minutes from the occasion to listen to some ideas from ISMC.

Bernard had jumped at the chance. He knew that Marion Charlotte would be there on his arm and the location was simply one of the best in London.

Today was the date and he was looking forward to meeting Marion Charlotte before the occasion. He had been given a Loft Terrace room in the nearby London Edition, which he knew was one of the finest boutique hotels in London. Now he was meeting Marion in the intimate Punch Room before they made their way into the restaurant.

He had taken a seat and was sipping his way through a rather delicious speciality gin and tonic. Marion arrived and he felt a frisson of energy as she walked into the bar. The casual unflappable barmen missed a beat as Marion walked in, noticed Driscoll and walked across to greet him.

"Darling, " she said, " How lovely to see you, I don't know about you but I'm looking forward to this dining experience!"

Bernard nodded agreement and then watched as Marion sat down. She was completely in control of her surroundings and a waiter moved over to ask her if she would like a drink.

"I'll have one of your lovely Champagnes, " she said, and Bernard watched in fascination as she briefly scanned the menu.

"Do you know what? Why don't you choose? Something for both of us?" She handed her menu to Bernard."

He looked along the delicious menu options and settled on one of the sharing selections. "There, he said triumphantly, how about this?"

She looked at his choice, " Er won't that come rather large?" she asked and pointed to a more slim-line section of the menu.

"I think I'd rather go for this lemon sole, " she said and maybe a mixed leaf to start?"

Bernard put away his thoughts of 'Buccleuch Estate chateaubriand, baby parsnips and wild mushrooms' and started to concentrate on the 'sea bream in lobster sauce' instead.

Then he heard voices outside of the room. In walked a man and a woman, whom Marion seemed to know. "Darlings, " she greeted them, " So glad you could make it, and this is Bernard Driscoll, the MP and Minister."

She hugged and kissed them both in what Bernard noticed was the same way that she greeted him.

"Hello Bernard, " said the man, who made to shake his hand. Bernard noticed it was a freemason's handshake. Quite elaborate, he recognised it as the lion's paw of a master mason.

"My name is Miller; Miller MacDonald, he said with a clearly American accent, and this is my friend Trudi Hartmann."

Driscoll looked towards Trudi, who was smiling back. She was another stunner, who, to Driscoll, looked like a young Claudia Schiffer.

"Delighted to meet you both, " answered Bernard, " Although I'm surprised because I thought Sir Charles Frobisher would be here?"

"Ah, Sir Charles, yes he is a good colleague of mine, said Miller, " We are both at ISMC, although you can probably tell from my accent that I'm based in America - in Texas, actually."

"Sir Charles was unavoidably detained this evening and

called to ask if I could take his place. Well I could hardly say no, what with such an awesome restaurant, two lovely ladies and a Member of Parliament for company!"

Bernard smiled.

"And I hear you like Formula One as well, I'm more of a NASCAR man, in The South you can't really avoid NASCAR and when I was younger, I lived in Dallas so the Texas Motor Speedway was never far away."

"I don't know so much about NASCAR, " said Bernard, " It seems to me that the drivers might get dizzy from only turning one way at the bends?"

"I know, they don't get paid quite as well as the Formula 1s, but to Southern ears it is reassuring to hear names like Earl, Jeff, Tony and Jimmie driving stink out of those cars."

"What instead of Max, Valtteri, Carlos, Sebastian, Fernando, Lewis, Jenson and Nico?" asked Driscoll, smiling, but feeling safe on one of his favourite topics."

"I used to be friends with Jamie Pollozini who is also a Formula One driver, " said Trudi, " His name sounds Italian, but he was from Perth in Australia, I remember he had an interesting nick-name."

"Oh, what was it?" asked Marion.

"I'll have to whisper, " said Trudi, " I know it's a bit rude to whisper, but so is the name." She stood, walked around the table to Marion's and whispered something in her ear. Then Marion whispered something back. They both laughed.

"Well, the girls seem to be having fun, " said Miller, " We boys need to have some too, but hey Darling, what shall we order? I'm thinking about the Chateaubriand?"

"You choose, " said Trudi, " So long as I can have it with Champagne."

The dinner proceeded and Driscoll came to see that Miller's exuberance somehow crossed into an altogether wilder side. Miller had tales of his sorority, of fishing in the Gulf of Mexico and of a penchant for classic sports cars. He was clearly well-heeled and well-travelled. In fact, Driscoll felt a little swamped by the anecdotes.

Then, Trudi excused herself from the table. Marion said she'd go along too.

That left the two men sitting across from one another.

"This is where the cigars would come out in my club in Austin. It's in a beautiful looking Antebellum building, with one of the few remaining statues of Robert E. Lee in the lobby. Most of Texas has now removed him from their memory, like some kind of Communist photo-coup. Yes, they took him off street signs, parks, pools and from the edges of the University in Atlanta. I'd put him as a smart man of his time. Opposed to slavery but accepting the social conditioning of the times which included 'be rude to slaves.' He also predicted that the war would be a long and bloody one."

Driscoll nodded. He didn't know much about the American Civil War, except the pieces he'd seen in that movie, what was it? Gone with the Wind. Burning of Atlanta. Sherman vs Hood. Someone set fire to the railroad boxcars of ammunition.

"Well, let's talk about something more modern, " said Miller, " I know you'll have been following the situation in Celarus. It's where we have a small ISMC outpost and where Raven are targeting to move Brant."

"Yes, said Driscoll, " Sir Charles referred to your presence when I met him the last time."

"I expect he mentioned the increased need to corral the effects around our bases. Like that situation in Iraq where the convoy was intercepted.

Miller looks at Bernard, " With you as the Minister for External Affairs, you can have a major influence on this and what happens next. The UK can either send politically sensitive troops into these areas, or with a little ingenuity can head off the problem, paving the way for infrastructure reconstruction and secure stability through the judicious sale of munitions.

Miller leaned towards Driscoll, " Your soft power influence behind the scene is all that is required to make this run along nicely. That's where we think you could be instrumental in stopping the violence and helping the trade position simultaneously.

Miller continued, " Bernard, this path provides opportunity for personal benefit without personal sacrifice."

Bernard was thinking; this was the second time he had heard ISMC make a similar offer.

"So, what, would I need to do?" he asked.

The Offer

"It's quite simple, really, " said Miller.

"Raven is divesting Qube. The recipient organisation is Brant, based in Brussels. There might be some challenges to this from Parliament, because it looks like another piece of Britain being sold off and too much like private security is running military situations."

Driscoll nodded. "No different from the Americans with their contractors running Basra and Helmand Province - DynCorp and Blackwater, to name but two. These keep coming across my desk."

"Admittedly so, but the situation with Qube is quite different, " said Miller, " It will be bidding fair and square for the construction contracts in Celarus and adding some value by building additional infrastructure within the original contract."

"Oh yes?" said Driscoll, " How can it afford to?"

"Quite simply, Risk and reward, Qube and soon-to-be Brant will have a tailored blend of military and construction expertise. Add that to the Raven energy knowledge and there's an unbeatable combination. We can construct bases and infrastructure as well as a new pipeline right across Celarus. It will completely deflect the Russian pipeline attempts to sell their energy to Europe."

"You said I'd be able to get some benefits from this?" asked Driscoll.

"Well there's two. One is purely reputational. You'll be the visionary that has seen the sense in the new endeavour and the benefits it brings to the British economy.

"Secondly, we plan to set up a kind of trust fund for you. It means you'll need a Driscoll Foundation or something which we can deposit money in. These won't be directly connected with your work as an MP but will be seen as an above-board humanitarian support for, say, the wellbeing of people in Celarus."

"What sort of deposits would we be talking about? " Asked Driscoll. "Well initially, maybe ten, to start it off. Then once the mechanism is established, we can look at maybe another couple each month. When the pipeline comes on stream, I guess that could increase, maybe to four."

"When you say 'ten' what do you mean, exactly, " asked Driscoll.

"Oh, sorry, ten million, I should have said, " answered Miller."

"And which currency are you describing?" asked Driscoll.

"Oh, sorry again - when in Britain - British Pounds, obviously."

"That's still quite a lot to take in."

"I guess that's all the upside, visionary fame and stealthy recompense. You'll need some sophisticated banking for this you realise, oh and don't worry about the Parliamentary speeches; we have some people that can help you with those."

"Is there any downside, apart from me discovering that I'm in an elaborate sting operation?" asked Driscoll.

"Well, yes, I should mention that too. How can I put this? There are not many people we have made these types of offer to. Those that accepted them are living very well. Those that didn't accept seem to have accidents soon after the offer was made."

"Ahah, now we get to it, a threat?" asked Driscoll.

"You could see it that way, or be like me, an optimist, and think of this leap of faith as one giant opportunity."

Parliamentary Debate

DIVESTMENT OF RAVEN CORPS
HC Deb 29 March cc1207-15

3.49 p.m.

The President of the Board of Trade
I beg to move, that this debate be conducted into the planned divestment from Raven Corps, of Qube into a new company based in London called Brant.

This is a short debate. It does not attempt to do everything, even in the field of monopolies, mergers and divestments.

It sets out to do what is most urgent and most necessary in the belief that we should not postpone doing anything until we can do everything.

The Minister for External Affairs (Bernard Driscoll)
The planned move is one part of the comprehensive

programme for streamlining and modernising British industry, which is crucial to the economic survival of this country, and which the Government are determined to launch.

If we are to retain, as I believe we must, a large sector of private enterprise in the mixed economy of this country, competition is essential as one safeguard of the efficiency and progressiveness of that private sector.

The Raven divestment is conceived in the belief, which I think is common to all parties, that monopolies, mergers and divestments are not always bad.

Sometimes they are and sometimes they are not.

This truth was admirably expressed in that classical document, which wears well with time, the White Paper on Employment Policy, of May, 1944—a bipartisan, perhaps I should say a tripartisan document which said that, although "arrangements or combines do not necessarily operate against the public interest", " nevertheless "the power to do so is there"."

1208

Three valid criticisms have been made of the working of our present dual system of a Monopolies Commission, on the one hand, and a Divestment Practices Court, on the other.

The first is that it has all been too slow. The Monopolies

Commission has not been able to work simultaneously on more than a very small number of inquiries; and each enquiry has tended to take years rather than months.

The watchdogs have barked, or prepared to bark, but meanwhile the monopolies have gone marching on.

We cannot let this situation arise for divestments, of which the Raven example if materially beneficial to the United Kingdom.

This situation breaks apart a behemoth, producing instead a more manageable beast and one that can be tamed by judicious oversight.

1209

But I should like to emphasise the value which we attach to the services of busy people in business and the professions who devote their time to this public work and to express our gratitude to them. [HON. MEMBERS: "Hear, hear."]

Where this firm (Raven) is really dominant in an important industry, controlling perhaps over half the market, we now have an ideal opportunity to see through changes which will reduce its size and potential impact within the control of the relevant sectors which it inhabits.

The smaller units produced - comprising a blend of Qube and Brant should be able to manage their new and diverse industry and successfully provide a positive Balance of Payments surplus to the United Kingdom.

Instead of an outflow of funding to the United States, we will see a new tax centre for Brant in London.

1210

Apart from those qualifications. however, I think that it is right that both professional and commercial services should be included within the scope of the divestment, though that does not, of course, mean that the Government have any present intention of rushing in to question the arrangements of the learned professions.

What the divestment does is to give the Government power to refer such commercial or professional practices to the Commission wherever this seems to be desirable and to use the powers contained in both the 1948 Act and the present Bill to restrain any practices which the Commission condemns.

1211

Mr. J. T. Spicer (West Loughton) Before my right hon. Friend leaves that point, in interpreting the intention of the Clause at a later stage will he pay particular attention to the effect on prices of cost accountancy and the very high fees which automatically are loaded in to inflated prices?

Mr. Driscoll I do not doubt that that is one of the

considerations which we shall take into account, but it is not necessarily the only one. I note, however, what my hon. Friend has said.

Many divestments, as I have said, will be positively in the national interest and can probably be reasonably easily seen to be so. Others, however, might tend, or, indeed, even be deliberately designed, to derail competition, which, in the last resort, is the only real justification of private enterprise. The practical problem, I think we should all agree, is to sift the one sort of divestment from the other
1212

Mr. A. E. Sopels (Ditherington-in-the Marsh, South) If a public announcement is made that two companies want to divest and re-form, and the Board of Trade decides that it wants to intervene, in what period of time would it make its decision? Because there could be a long period of uncertainty while there was dithering in the Board of Trade.

Mr. Driscoll I am coming in a moment to the point of what the Board of Trade would do if a proposition of that sort were put to it.

I believe that the legal powers embodied in the Bill are sufficiently flexible in that they leave it possible for divestments to go forward in many cases with no investigation at all, but also provide for investigation either before or after the event as may seem desirable.

Even, of course, when the Commission has inquired, and made its report, it will still be possible for the President of the Board of Trade of the day, who, I think, as responsible to this House, must be the final judge, short of Parliament itself, to accept or to reject the Commission's recommendations, but when action is clearly shown to be necessary Parliament will have the power, by affirmative Order, to prohibit or dissolve a divestment found by the Commission to be contrary to the public interest.

Next—and I come to the hon. Gentleman's question—the House may reasonably ask what criteria the Board of Trade will use in deciding which divestments should be referred to the Commission and which should be left alone.

1213

We have given some thought already to this question. Mergers are of very great variety, and I do not propose to attempt to spell out precisely the cases where the public interest might be at risk. One obvious case, I think, is where competition in a vital industry might be markedly reduced.

That is why we have provided, as an alternative to the criterion of monopoly, a size of assets test, so that what are called vertical or diversifying mergers could be investigated if the public interest required.

Divestments involving large firms are not, of course,

necessarily harmful to the public interest. In judging all these cases, however, I would propose always to remember what divestment in certain cases can do to achieve greater strength for our economy at home and abroad.

1214

Sir John Cricklewood (Seven-Teeseoak and Gomply-Titheridge) Would the right hon. Gentleman say, for the purpose of clarification, whether the powers he has outlined apply not only to divestments covered by the Measure, but also to divestments voluntarily negotiated?

Mr. Driscoll Yes, certainly. They apply in either case where divestment would be the result of the operation.

Mr. A. Cokeburner (Dopley and South Trumsett) May I put a question to my right hon. Friend on that? My right hon. Friend will remember that one of the large items which gave rise to a good deal of agitation was big accounting firm divestments. Would those come under the scheme?

1215

Mr. Driscoll Yes, certainly. This is ground-breaking for a divestment but others may follow a similar path.

Forward to ROYAL ASSSENT
Noticed a typo? | Report other issues DIVESTMENT OF RAVEN CORPS
HC Deb 29 March cc1207-15

The Launch

"It's happening, " said Bigsy, " The divestment of Qube."

"They are setting up Brant just like your friend said, Christina."

"What, Elena?" said Christina, " That seems like such a long time ago."

"The mills of the gods grind slowly, but they grind exceeding fine, " chipped in Clare.

"I'm not so sure about that, " said Christina, " Where I come from the Gods can be pretty fiery tempered and run around wielding big hammers."

Jake continued, " Well anyway, it looks as if Driscoll has fronted the deal through a debate in Parliament. They've a green flag now to go ahead and split off Qube from Raven and to amalgamate it with Brant, just like Elena predicted. Another British Company becomes

European."

Bigsy added, " Then remember what Nelson said, they will get rid of the people from Raven that have been transferred to Brant and start afresh with a new team. It's a classic outsourcer manoeuvre."

"So, is this some kind of Masonic move?" asked Clare, looking towards Jake, " Or is it something else?"

"It smacks of *Vzyatochnichestvo* - that's corrupt practices, " said Christina, " In Russian, we say блат *(blat)* , which is a is a form of corruption through a system of informal agreements, exchanges of services, connections, Party contacts, or black market deals to achieve results or get ahead.

"The *blatnoy (блатной)* run much of the *blat*. It has a criminal meaning in Russian and it relates to a status in the criminal world. It usually means a member of a thief gang, *(blatnoy/блатной)* itself means professional criminal in Russian."

"So, you are not saying the Russians are involved in this?" asked Bigsy, looking concerned.

"No, just that this corruption is as old as the hills. You English say 'You scratch my back, I scratch yours.' In Russian we say 'One hand washes the other,' " said Christina making her hands make a washing gesture.

"But the other thing is, if this was blat, there would be more to it. Split off the company, move the people, set-up a new boss structure. But you have to ask the question, Why? " said Christina.

"You think there is more to it?" asked Jake.

"There must be, " said Christina, " Someone is out to make a lot of money or secure a huge amount of power, otherwise why entrap Driscoll? Why set up that Minerva station?"

Financial Times

"Look here, " said Bigsy, " The FT is calling the Qube divestment from Raven creating Brant a financial triumph. Raven's shares went up by 7% and the Brant shares are already trading at nearly 2x their original predicted level.

"Think about that for a minute, " said Jake, " All the advisors and financiers to that deal will have underwritten it to some degree. The Brotherhood will all be coining it in."

Bigsy added, " The deal is led by Lucy Sidwell, from Raven's Corporate Treasury, she is a Board Member, but I seriously doubt that she would be a Mason."

"Yes, but there has to be another move behind the divestment, " said Christina. "Trust me, I've run security for too many of these kinds of operations."

Jakes's phone rang. "Oh, hello Amanda. How are you? Yes, it has been a while. Yes, Chuck did say you might call."

Jake walked to the whiteboard and wrote Amanda Miller in big letters.

"Yes, Yes, we were. I know, we saw it too. As a matter of fact, we were just talking about it."

"When? What topic? This isn't a hoax of anything?"

"Okay, I'll ask the others and ring you back. Goodbye then. Until later!"

He switched off his phone.

"Well that is an interesting development, " said Jake, " It was Amanda Miller from SI6. You remember when she detained me that time you - Clare and Bigsy - were gallivanting around Arizona?"

"Well she's been tracking the developments on Brant too and wants to talk. She mentioned something about a politician."

"Interesting, " said Christina, " Although I'm not sure I should be present. I get the feeling Amanda would feel the need to turn me in to some of her associates."

"I seriously doubt it, " said Jake, " I expect Amanda will treat you in the same way the Chuck did. Kind of Case Closed - based upon that other Russian name - what was it? Vanonin?

"Voronin, " corrected Clare.

"Okay, we'll all go then," said Jake, " I'll suggest to Amanda that we meet at the Riverfront, by the book sellers. It's a kind of classic spy movie setting, " said Jake.

"Not to mention Hugh Grant and Andie MacDowell in Four Weddings and a Funeral, " added Clare.

"Game on, " said Jake.

Four Theories and a Funeral

*"You come to nature with all your theories,
and she knocks them all flat."*

— Renoir

The Riverside

Amanda was already sitting at one of the small outside tables when Clare, Bigsy, Jake and Christina arrived.

"Wow, I get to meet you all!" said Amanda, " I know Jake from way back, but I think a couple of you were travelling around the American deserts when we were last involved together."

They all shook hands and introduced themselves. Bigsy made his way inside to buy some coffees.

"Clare and Bigsy, I've heard of, but I don't think I know you, Christina?"

"You might know me by other names, but we'll keep it simple today, " said Christina.

"You are not Voronin? Katarina Voronin?" asked Amanda, " Chuck was mighty respectful of you if that's the case! I seem to remember we captured you somewhere, and the case got closed?"

"That's more or less the same story that Chuck remembered, " said Christina, " But I can see I'll need another name change after this operation is complete."

Amanda paused looked closely at Christina and said, " Yes but the Archangel name will follow you around. I'm in the presence of a super-agent."

Christina smiled. It was good to know her reputation was even visible in London.

"They made part of Four Weddings and a Funeral outside here, " said Amanda. Jake and Clare nodded.

"Hugh Grant and Andie MacDowell, " answered Clare, " With Kristin Scott Thomas!"

"Yes - I hear you've moved to a new office?" asked Amanda, " After your other one was fire-bombed?"

"That's right, " said Jake, " Although we are keeping the exact circumstances reasonably low key for the insurance."

"So how could we be of assistance?" asked Jake.

"Look, I know you know Chuck Manners and he suggested that I contact you about all of this. I gather you have found an American Station working out of Canada Water, but outsourced to Qube- nowadays Brant? And that you've noticed something untoward about Bernard Driscoll?

"The American Station is, we think, the source of the fire-bomb to our offices. We think it was an American incendiary grenade. We suspect Qube of having a hand in it."

"Then Driscoll, we think someone is operating him to smooth the divestment from Raven of Qube to Brant. And we also think that it hasn't played out yet. We think there is something else in the works."

Amanda nodded, " I've been drawing the same conclusions. There's some heavy-handed Freemasonry in the mix, but I think that is just to camouflage whatever Driscoll is doing."

"You'll know he has been seen around Freemason parties lately, and heading off into small smoke-filled rooms?"

"We'd heard about some of this but can't tie it together."

"We think that Raven is pulling some of the strings here. American interests moving to make money from civil unrest. You know the model. Sell them weapons. Architect the unrest. Sell them peacekeeping. Sell them reparations. Harvest whatever natural resources they have.

"Syria is a case in point. It's a long time since the ceasefires, yet the embedded industries of Qube are still present. Occasional little skirmishes break out which prevent the US from pulling out completely.

"Now it seems to be positioning for Celarus. Brant are already present there.

"With the divestment/merger we can see Brant establishing a presence. Just as a few arguments break out along the border. It will be the usual American response. Fly some planes along to knock out perimeter defences. Then America will want to build a base. Do they build their own? Hell No. They get some builder in to do the hard work, building roads and MacDonald's cafeterias for the troops. Maybe an airfield and a few other security measures.

"Who will they call? Why Brant of course. Next things we see is Brant's share price rocketing as they land some big fat American orders for defence infrastructure. And if America can persuade a few NATO Allies to join in, then why wouldn't they use the incumbent suppliers?

"Ker-ching, " said Bigsy.

"Exactly, " said Amanda, " So you could say I'm eager to trace the lineage of the Brant deal up the chain of command. I can get as far as Driscoll, but then it stops.

"Well Driscoll has some weaknesses for 'the ladies' , " said Christina, " I met him at a Freemason Ladies' Night. I also met a couple of other escorts and was told about their head of arrangements, someone named Jennifer Sussex. "

"That's great, " said Amanda, " We can chase that link through. Try to pin Driscoll down."

"Do you think he's being rewarded for what he is doing?" asked Clare.

"Oh yes, he must be, and likely it is very well recompensed, " answered Christina, " The sort of deals I saw, the slush funds were immense."

"So, what's the move to be?" asked Clare.

"Do what we'd do. Scare him and turn him, " said Christina.

Popups

Bigsy's computer went into meltdown after he typed in the search for 'London Escort Agencies.'

He was trying to find the elusive Jennifer, or a link to any of the other women that had been present at the Ladies Night.

He'd drawn a complete blank, although he now had a comprehensive folder of potentially scary future dates.

Jake and Clare thought it hilarious, not to mention the range of new search terms that Bigsy seemed to have acquired.

"All of those little sidebar and popup adverts have changed from USB gadgets and back pain remedies to 'ladies looking for lurve,' " he added.

Amanda decided to use her contacts with GCHQ to try to trace what was happening in Celarus.

Grace had put together a briefing profile.

It was simple. The Celarus government was fragile. Their leader was under attack from the opposition and they were trying to encourage military leaders to join the new breakaway movement.

In the middle of this, Brant were building a new base for the Americans and the Americans in turn were providing security services to the Celarusian government.

It was rumoured that there was a massive pipeline deal in the works too and that Brant were front-runner for the construction.

"We've all the pieces, " said Amanda.

"I think we can add on something personal - there's his wife and daughter out in Norfolk. I doubt they know about Bernard's dalliances."

"Nor would they think him capable, " added Grace.

They both laughed.

"So how do we lure him for a meeting?" Asked Grace.

"He seems keen on the women, so I guess a conventional honey trap might be the way to go, " said Amanda.

"Won't he be suspicious?" asked Grace.

"He thinks of himself has a powerful man. What do they like to surround themselves with?"

"Oh okay, let's run with it, but whom?"

"Well, we could start with Marion Charlotte, I suppose, assuming she is more coin-operated than loyal to her prior masters?"

"Do you think he'd be suspicious of a call from her?"

"I think the only way to find out will be to approach her. We'll need some theatrics around it too."

Using Grace's links in GCHQ, they soon tracked down a London address for Marion Charlotte. Amanda planned a direct head-to-head confrontation with her.

Vzyatochnichestvo

Marion Charlotte's address was a smart building in West London. It was in a street of similar looking four story tall white painted building with huge pillars either side of a grand looking porch.

Amanda considered using SI6 for the approach, but felt, on balance that it would bet better to use someone from the Triangle offices. It would improve subsequent deniability and stopped any rumour from circulating that Driscoll was being investigated.

The Triangle team had decided that Christina would accompany Amanda, although they realised that this was a surprise twinning of a SI6 office with someone from FSB.

"Don't worry, " said Christina, I'll be scary if required."

They were outside the house and Amanda rang a bell which had neatly printed the name M Charlotte.

"Hello, " called the entry system, " who is there?"

"Hello, we are friends of Bernard Driscoll, " answered

Amanda, " We come about the secret party we want to throw for him."

"Second Floor, " came the reply and a buzz.

They were in and would meet Marion Charlotte in a few moments.

"Come in, " said Marion. They entered an opulent and tidy realm. Fashionable pictures on the walls, decorative walls and sumptuous furnishings. It reminded Amanda of a cover-shoot.

"A glass of wine, maybe?" asked Marion.

"I'm surprised you have been able to find me here, I'm not even sure that Bernard has this address?"

"We got it from Jennifer, " replied Christina.

"Ah okay, I see, " said Marion, " She is not supposed to give it out. Security and all."

"Well we thought this was a special situation, " said Amanda, " We want to surprise Bernard, " based upon some of the little things he's been up to lately, " we want to offer him a big bonus."

"Oh, I see, " said Marion, " To be honest, if you want me to call him, you'll have been told my rates by Jennifer at MDA. I'm inclined to add surge rates for Driscoll though."

All three laughed at the reference to Uber's peak charging policy.

"So, what would it take to get you to invite him to what I

promise will be a surprise party?" asked Christina.

"I'll write it down, " said Marion. She found some paper and a pen and wrote down what seemed to Amanda to be an excessive sum.

"Half in front and half after the deal?" asked Christina, " direct payments?"

"That will do nicely, " said Marion.

Gavvers

Marion had invited Driscoll to her surprise event. She was sure he had come along. She had told him it was a small private party to celebrate winning a modest award and that he would be her partner.

She had told him it was lounge suits and not very formal. They were meeting at La Gavroche in Upper Brook Street and would be dining in the Chef's Library.

Driscoll could hardly believe his luck that he was now being invited out by the lovely Marion. And this sounded like a more intimate session that some of the others which had a certain working bias.

Now that his Foundation was up-and-running and seemed to be accumulating a decent bankroll, he felt quite positive about all of this.

He arrived at La Gavroche and was shown through to the Chef's Library. It included an intimate banquette and table and looked as if it would hold about six people. He wondered who the others would be.

Marion was next to arrive, they greeted one another, and

she sat next to him in the centre of the banquette.

"Who are we waiting for?" asked Bernard.

"Oh, you'll see, soon enough, " twinkled Marion.

They could hear footsteps from a small group and then four people entered, two men in suits and two pretty women.

"Here we are, all ready for the surprise!" said Marion.

The others moved forward to introduce themselves, Amanda Miller, Christina Hyde, Jake Lambers and Dave Shelley- but you can call me Bigsy."

"Champers all around?" enquired Driscoll.

"Now that's what I call an ice-breaker, " said Jake.

They sat around the rest of the banquette and on two smaller chairs directly opposite to Driscoll and Marion. Christina and Amanda were directly facing Marion and Driscoll.

"We haven't got the boy-girl thing quite right, " quipped Jake.

"No, this is fine, " said Christina.

"I remember you!" said Driscoll, " You were at the Ladies' Night at the Raven Hall? - You were on Gerhardt's table; I think you wore a deep blue gown."

Christina was silently pleased that the von Fürstenberg was still working its magic, even after all of this time.

"That's right, " she said, and pointedly looked towards her small rose brooch, the one that Antanov had given her, " I seem to remember that you were called away for a meeting with Sir Charles Frobisher?"

"Oh, you know Sir Charles?" asked Driscoll, unaware that anything was amiss. By now he had seen the rose and now noticed the symbolism of the triangular background.

He had been looking through those books that Gerhardt had provided. That symbol that Christina wore. It was The Ancient Mystical Order Rosae Crucis - AMORC. He was in the presence of someone well-connected.

He remembered that there was no religious connotation associated with this symbol; the Rose Cross symbol predated Christianity. The cross symbolized the human body and the rose represented the individual's unfolding consciousness.

"I can see you looking at the brooch, " said Christina, aware that Driscoll was once again staring at her for just too long.

She continued, "It has quite a history, dating back to 1500BC. It taps into a special gnosis, a secret wisdom. Thousands of years ago in ancient Egypt select bodies or schools were formed to explore the mysteries of life and learn the secrets of this hidden wisdom."

"Fascinating, " said Driscoll, " But I thought women could not reach higher degrees in the Masons?"

The waiter arrived. He introduced the dinner. Brought along some canapés. It was to be a tasting menu, matched with a sommelier choice of fine wines.

"You miss the point, Bernard, " said Christina, toughening her speech. "Together, the rose and cross represent the experiences and challenges of a thoughtful life well lived.

"Thus, by our name and symbol we stand for the ancient fraternity of Rosicrucians, perpetuating the true traditions of Rosicrucian movements from centuries past to the present day."

Amanda looked at Christina, she was a little startled that Christina appeared to know so much.

"Yes, said Jake, " The further one travels, the less one knows."

"That'd be George Harrison, " said Bigsy, sipping lightly at the freshly delivered champagne cocktails, " The Inner Light."

"Yes, said Jake, " Now Mr Driscoll, Bernard - we must decide whether to look within you, or whether we are better without you, " said Jake, riffing on the Beatles tunes.

Amanda cut in, " Bernard Driscoll, we have reason to suspect that you may be in breach of the Official Secrets Act, on several counts, which include:

"Conspiring to manipulate political events for personal gain;

"Creating a tax haven vehicle for the deposit of funds from a foreign undeclared source;

"Leaking government plans to a commercial enterprise;

"Manipulating bids to elicit a favourable outcome for a pre-selected supplier;

"Speaking, in Parliament, to pre-condition a foreign divestment for personal gain.

"This is preposterous, " interrupted Driscoll, " Marion, do you know anything about any of this?"

"Yes darling, I do, " she said, " surely you remember some of those conversations you had, with Raven Corps?"

The waiter reappeared. "Consommé de Volaille et Sot-l'y-laisse aux Epices d'Asie

That is Chicken Oysters and Broth flavoured with Asian Spices, " he announced.

Amanda cut in, " But then, Bernard, to our amazement, you set up the external foundation. You didn't make it too difficult for us, did you, Bernard? - Imagine naming it The Driscoll Foundation!? - Nothing like making it easy to cross-check."

"But I put that Foundation in Lichtenstein, " answered Driscoll, " Where it was assured of privacy."

Amanda replied, " Maybe you did, but the payments into your UBS account, held by the Foundation were sufficiently easy to cross check."

Amanda pulled a small black book from her bag. She opened it and read:

"Let us summarise - You received £10 million initially and then seem to have a £2 million run-rate. But the clincher is another set of payments. These all coincide with payments to Brant. The new American base in Celarus. The deal was for $234m, then the perimeter management $68 million and finally the new riverside docks was $48 million. Your Foundation has received, concurrently, $2.34 million, $0.68 million and $0.48 million."

Driscoll looked rattled.

"What if I deny everything?" he said.

"Well, the recording that Bigsy here is making won't go down so well in a Crown Court or The Old Bailey, I admit, but it will work just fine in my offices at SI6, " said Amanda.

Driscoll looked as if he was getting ready to make a dash for it, except he was sandwiched between several people around the table.

"Look, don't think about running, " said Christina, " I can do 100 metres in 11 seconds, although maybe not in these heels. But I am also quite accurate with a knife. Even one of these." She picked up a steak knife.

The waiter had been busy, and the next course arrived, " Salsifi Roti au Beurre et Amandes Salees - That's Whole Roast Salsify with Spanish Salted Almonds and Cornish Smoked Sea Salt, " he announced triumphantly.

Driscoll's chest sank. He could see he had been outsmarted.

"Will you be telling my wife about this?" he asked.

They looked at one another, Jake almost laughed. Even Marion smirked.

Amanda looked towards Driscoll, " Look, we know you've been duped. You will probably get a sentence of something like 30 years for this. But we are more interested in the even bigger players. I've a deal for you."

"I'm interested, " said Driscoll.

Christina was amazed at how quickly Driscoll had folded.

"Okay, you'll need to work your way up the chain of command. Who is the next level? Who gives you instructions?"

"I can already answer both of those, " said Driscoll, " Sir Charles Frobisher and then Michael Tovey, the MP - They wield significant influence in all of this."

"Okay, said Amanda, " We'll have to treat you as a mole."

"Mole? " Said Driscoll.

"It sounds better than a snitch, " said Bigsy.

"Yes, we will want to know what your organisation is planning, so that when needed we can run countermeasures. What you are doing amounts to terrorism. You are using clandestine means to subvert the course of the British Government."

The waiter looked interestedly at the group, as if he was

trying to work out whether they were playing an elaborate game of Murder Mystery, " Saumon Marnine et Fume aux Sirop d'Erable that's Maple Cured and Hot Smoked Var Salmon with Crème Fraiche, Dill, Gherkin and Pickled Shallots."

Driscoll said, " I'd still need to look as if I was gaining from this."

"Agreed, " said Amanda, " but the UBS funds will be re-routed to an SI6 suspense account. You cannot be seen to profit from this."

"So, the price of my freedom is to turn me into a double agent?" asked Driscoll.

"That's right, " said Amanda, " But on this occasion you will be ideology free."

Jake and Bigsy looked at one another. They were both thinking that Amanda had just told Driscoll he was vacuous.

The waiter returned again, " Selle de Cabri Roti Jus au Thym et Olives - this time we present Roast Saddle of Somerset Kid Goat, Thyme Jus and Provencal Garnish."

Amanda continued, " Look and don't think you'll be able to wriggle out of this once you are back on Upper Brook Street. We've folk who can track you down very easily and we'd soon know if you were attempting an identity change."

There was pause.

"You know, this is really good food, " said Bigsy, " and

the pudding is still to come."

"I'll want this tied down legally, " said Driscoll, " You make me an offer and I accept it and with it your ongoing protection."

"I'll have to see what we can arrange through SI6, " said Amanda.

"Vzaimnykh a ne Vzyatochnichestvo" said Christina, making a slight Russian pun of the words for reciprocity and bribery. She noticed something. That Marion appeared to chuckle too.

The waiter returned again, " Ossau Irraty aux Truffes and Cerises. That's Layered Ossau Irraty and Truffles, Cherry Compote and Walnut Bread"

"Wow, now for the cheese!" said Bigsy.

"Yeah, its sheep's milk cheese too, " said Jake.

"It must be strange, how some of us can enjoy this meal, whilst others are finding it difficult to swallow, " said Amanda, " I must say that this is delicious, and with the wine, well - sublime."

"I think I'll save myself for the French Toast, " said Jake. They had all noticed that Bernard's usually healthy appetite had, on this occasion, run out. He was leaving course after course of the food, although he seemed capable of consuming the wine.

"That's a good point, " said Christina, I think we should have a toast now, to celebrate our new understandings,

"May we suffer as much sorrow as drops of wine we are

about to leave in our glasses!"

"Wow, said Jake, That's a bit heavy!

"Slavic, " said Christina.

"*Poyekhali!*" said Amanda, " See, I know a Russian toast too!"

"Em, that means 'Let's get started', or 'Go!' You'd normally say that at the start of a meal, not the end, " said Christina, " It was well-pronounced though, " She looked towards Marion who nodded agreement.

"Look and now here comes a French toast, " said Jake as the waiter re-appeared.

"The gentleman is correct; this is Pain Perdu, Rhubarbe et Gingembre - that is Glazed French Toast with Yorkshire Rhubarb and Crystalized Ginger, " said the waiter.

"Perhaps you could bring us some coffees now, please?" asked Jake.

"Certainly, " said the waiter, " The coffee comes with Petit Fours comprising Sable Breton, Apple and Cinnamon, Pate de Fruit, Extra Bitter Chocolate."

Amanda looked around the table.

Thanks to her renewed acquaintances and a resting FSB agent, they had caught a corrupt Cabinet Minister who was selling UK diplomatic positions for a grubby commercial gain. She mused that it could even be classed as treason.

She felt pleased with herself that they were even able to turn the situation to an advantageous one, where Driscoll would become a mole for the UK Government.

Wrap it up

They had reassembled at the temporary Triangle offices near Bishopsgate.

Christina, Bigsy, Clare and Jake were seated around a table.

"I think that ended well, " said Jake, " We managed to track down and stop a corporation that are doing bad things."

"Yes, because of the bribery of that rather sleazy Bernard Driscoll, " added Clare.

"And under the cover of the Freemasons, " said Christina.

"Have you seen this?" said Bigsy.

He held up the Daily Telegraph.

"I didn't know you could read, not from paper anyway?"

said Jake.

"Ha-Ha - No, Look- Seriously, " said Bigsy, he pointed to an article on the front page. 'Cabinet Minister in Fatal Car Crash'

Bigsy continued, " It says that Bernard Driscoll was on his way from his constituency to his family home, when his car suffered a puncture and crashed off the road, into a ditch, hitting an electricity sub-station. According to the police reports he was not wearing a seat belt and they found that his phone was on, although the number was International. They are calling it death by misadventure."

Christina looked up, " I wondered, you know, that we kept Marion Charlotte in for the whole dinner. I could not quite place it, but I thought she noticed a couple of things that I wouldn't expect. When I spoke Russian and when Amanda did, I could see her look of recognition. I think we were played."

"What? Do you think that Marion was still actively working for Raven?" asked Bigsy.

Christina answered, " If so, then she would know that Driscoll was compromised. She could tell Raven. They could clean up after Driscoll's mistakes.

They had got what they wanted from him. And removing him would mean they didn't have to pay him any longer. But now I'm concerned there seems to be a Russian angle on this."

Jake said, " We'd better call Amanda Miller then and warn her. She would also be compromised."

"If there is a Russian angle, then I think it is organised crime rather than pure state, " said Christina,

" Russian organized crime or Russian mafia (российская мафия) otherwise known as Bratva (братва).

It is a collective of various organized crime elements.

Today, there are as many as 6,000 different groups, with more than 200 of them having a global reach.

"Criminals of these groups are often former prison members, corrupt officials and business leaders, people with ethnic ties, or people from the same region with shared criminal experiences and leaders. Some claim it is one of the best structured criminal organizations in Europe, with a quasi-military operation. Some say they are operating puppets in the White House.

"So, the Americans are pushing to get Raven installed in Celarus, under the name Brant. But you think there may be Russian influences there too?" said Bigsy, " That's one hell of a hot-spot".

Christina said, " Yes, I think we stumbled into something altogether more malevolent. I now have a feeling that Marion is about to disappear. If she was trained the way I've been trained, then she would know she was 'burned' and already be calling the FSB for a new identity."

"We'll need to take heed too and maybe lose our connections with this entire situation."

"Yes, at least you've been able to operate as unknown freelancers in all of this.

"It's people like Chuck, Amanda and me that get the scrutiny. We are the ones that people will watch."

Loud and clear

Sir Charles Frobisher sat in his ISMC office at Raven Corps.

"Interesting, " he said, " How useful to get a microphone into their temporary office."

www.ingramcontent.com/pod-product-compliance
Lightning Source LLC
Chambersburg PA
CBHW071330080526
44587CB00017B/2791